W9-BNT-039

The Truth About

MASONS

Robert Morey

HARVEST HOUSE PUBLISHERS
Eugene, Oregon 97402

THE TRUTH ABOUT MASONS
formerly *The Origins and Teachings of Freemasonry*

Copyright © 1993 by Robert Morey
Published by Harvest House Publishers
Eugene, Oregon 97402

Library of Congress Cataloging-in-Publication Data

Morey, Robert A., 1946– .
    The truth about masons / Robert Morey.
      p.   cm.
    Rev. ed. of: The origins and teachings of freemasonry.
    ISBN 1-56507-077-1
    1. Freemasonry—Religious aspects—Christianity. 2. Free-
masonry—United States—History. I. Morey, Robert A., 1946-   Origins and
teachings of freemasonry. II. Title.
HS495.M67   1993
366'.1—dc20   92-27372
                                                          CIP

Printed in the United States of America.

Special thanks to:

The Head Librarian of the
House of the Temple, Washington, D.C
and the Grand Lodge
of Pennsylvania, Philadelphia.

About the Author

Dr. Morey is the Executive Director of the Research and Education Foundation and the author of over 20 books, some of which have been translated into French, German, Spanish, Dutch, Italian, Finnish, Polish, and Chinese. He is an internationally recognized scholar in the field of comparative religions, the cults, and the occult.

The Research and Education Foundation is dedicated to investigating topics which affect Western culture and values. For a catalog of all of Dr. Morey's books and tapes write to: The Research and Education Foundation, P.O. Box 141455, Austin, Texas 78714.

CONTENTS

INTRODUCTION

The subject of Freemasonry is of interest to Masons and non-Masons alike. When and where did Masonry begin? What were the first Masons like? What were their beliefs? What did they say about the origins of Freemasonry? Is modern Freemasonry faithful to the original goal and vision of the founders of Masonry?

Such questions as these deserve a solid answer that is based on hard evidence. But the average Masonic book today which deals with such issues is based on pure speculation and an overactive imagination. These books are so contradictory of each other that they produce a great deal of confusion.

So much misinformation has been given about the history and teachings of the Fraternity that no one seems to know what the truth is anymore. It seems that modern writers vie with each other in trying to see who can give the weirdest interpretation of the symbols and rituals of the Craft. It almost seems that the wilder the claim, the more it is believed!

Are there any Masons left who just want the truth, plain and simple, without any wild or weird ideas? We believe that there are millions of honest Masons who are fed up with all the lies and falsehoods told and retold about the origins and teachings of Masonry.

They are tired of hearing about some pagan mystery religion from "the dawn of time" that is supposed to be the true religion of Freemasonry.

They are tired of being fed the same old line that the ancient mysteries, the druids, the Mayans, the Hindus, etc., are the "secret" origins of Freemasonry when no one has ever come up with a shred of evidence to support such claims.

There are millions of Masons who ask themselves why can't Masonry be a fraternal organization and that is all? Why do they have to be druid priests as some Masonic writers claim?

Is it not time for someone to write an objective hard-hitting book which tells it like it is? A book that does not spare even the "sacred cows" of Freemasonry in its search for the truth?

This is the motivation which drove us to research hundreds of Masonic books on the origins and teachings of Freemasonry. It fell to us to cut the Gordian knot of Masonic legend and lore. This was not an easy task. We had to separate fact from fiction, truth from error, and history from fantasy. It meant that we had to ask repeatedly what the evidence was for this or that claim.

Cherished ideas had to be placed on the rubbish heap of false ideas. Nothing was sacred or exempt from the light of rational investigation. The truth was the beginning and the end of our search.

In order that all the members of the Fraternity may feel the force of the truth about the origins and teaching of the Craft, *only Masonic writers will be quoted in this book*. While no anti-Masons or outside authorities will be cited in the text, we will put such information in the footnotes at the end of each chapter for those who wish outside confirmation.

This book is dedicated to all honest Masons who want to know the truth about the origins and teachings of Freemasonry. After all, the truth is never afraid of the searching light of historical research. The truth sets us free from ignorance and error. Thus the wise will always welcome truth wherever they find it.

The Truth About
About
MASONS

1

OPENING
PRINCIPLES

I t will be helpful for the reader to understand at the very beginning of this book the scientific principles which we have followed in our study of the origins and history of Freemasonry. In this way, the reader will know *how* we arrived at our conclusions as well as what we found.

It is a shame that past writers on Freemasonry did not begin by carefully thinking through what methodology they would be using in their research. The most atrocious things have been said both in favor of and against Freemasonry which arose out of a false methodology. Conclusions have been reached which are patently false or ridiculous. Most Masonic and anti-Masonic writers are equally guilty of these things.

Not only must we deal with poor research, but bias and prejudice has blinded many writers to any evidence that would tend to undermine their cherished views. Prejudice also has the nasty habit of twisting the evidence to prove a point or to make an attack on someone's motives. Hence the origins of most anti-Masonic "hate" literature that has produced more heat than light.

The First Principle

We should be as objective and factual as humanly possible. After all, what we all want is the *truth*. Thus our research should not reflect any "axes to grind" or causes to champion. We should not hold any malice toward Masons or anti-Masons alike.

The Second Principle

We must be so committed to the truth that we will follow the evidence no matter where it leads. This becomes painful when cherished beliefs and prejudices are shown to be false.

The Third Principle

Only verifiable historical evidence will be trusted. Legends, myths, speculations, guesswork, hearsay and traditions are so unreliable that they are worthless.

The Fourth Principle

Since Masonic writers have by and large indulged in much fantasy and fraud, when it comes to Freemasonry before 1717, their statements cannot be taken at face value. They have not hesitated to manufacture "ancient" documents when needed or to insert Masonic words or phrases in ancient manuscripts. Their works must be taken with the proverbial "grain of salt."

Albert Mackey, who was not himself guiltless in this regard, viewed with disdain the Masonic writers who went before him. In dealing with the so-called "Antiquity Manuscript" quoted by Preston, Hughan, etc., Mackey complains,

> Here we have evidence of a criminal inaccuracy of the Masonic writers of the last century, who never hesitated to alter or to interpolate passages in old documents whenever it was required to confirm a preconceived theory.[1]

We will quote Mackey and other Masonic writers when there is sufficient hard evidence to back up their statements. But when they begin to speculate out of thin air, this is when we part company.

Some of the more reliable twentieth-century Masonic writers have confirmed the basic unreliability of eighteenth- and nineteenth-century Masonic historians. One such writer by the name of A. S. Macbride comments,

> In no branch of history is care and judgment more needful than in that of Masonry. Nowhere else will you find such a collection of mendacious tales, such outrages on truth and common sense, as in the so-called histories of Anderson, Preston, Laurie, and some other writers. These publications have created contempt in the minds of non-Mason critics, not only for the authors but also for Masonry itself, and, no doubt, this is the reason why historians generally neglect the Masonic field. Within the Order, unfortunately, these histories, until recently, were accepted as real by the bulk of its members. The bald and bold assertions and unverified claims that crowd their pages were received

as gospel; and, as usual with such unreasonable beliefs, they developed fanatical bigotry. To cast doubt on their absolute truthfulness was anathema. This blind credulity created a natural reaction of skepticism and unbelief in the minds of many intelligent members. The beautiful symbolism and noble principles of Masonry were dragged into the gutter by these false historic pretentions, and its ceremonies were made to appear as sham and make-believe comedy.[2]

Melvin Johnson, who is still held in high esteem by many Masons, was not afraid to point out the unreliability of his fellow Masonic writers.

Some assertions concerning the early history of Freemasonry in the Western Hemisphere, utterly unwarranted and without a shred of justification, have been so publicly made heretofore and copied and recopied by serious Masonic scholars even as late as the current year, as to demand notice here so that the future student shall not be misled as Gould, Hughan, and others have been. Concerning some of them, I shall speak very plainly. Nothing can justify the deliberate concealment of a reliable document or the publication of that which is manifestly fraudulent for the purpose of bolstering up an argument in behalf of some pet theory which the Fraternity is asked to believe.[3]

Too many so-called Masonic historians since the days when they should have known better have added fiction to fable and imagination to both, using the manifest errors of their predecessors as gospel, dreams as evidence, and guesses as proof. Moreover, we must confess that there are many speakers and writers on Masonic subjects today who do not seem to realize that such methods do our cause more harm than good.[4]

... the Masonic historian should be subject to the same tests of accuracy as all other historians... But dreamland and the "wish that is father to the thought" must not be permitted [any] longer to influence the writing of what purports to be real history.[5]

Delmar Darrah, whose work on the behalf of Freemasonry cannot be questioned, was honest enough to state that,

In the realm of Freemasonry, there has been much of the enchantment of imagination. Masons have believed the things concerning the origin of the institution that they wanted to believe and have gone forth and told them as facts. When links were missing, they have been supplied by drawing upon fertile imaginations... So a good many Masonic writers and speakers have located the beginnings of Freemasonry so many thousands of years ago as to exempt the society from all natural laws.[6]

The first books written upon Freemasonry and which, for a long time served to guide the Craft, have no historical value whatsoever. They were simply the result of ambitious Masonic historians who knew little of the real development of the Fraternity and who relied solely upon their imagination to create a fiction which they panned off as the legitimate history of the Craft.[7]

It has been charged that the compilation

of landmarks as presented by Dr. Mackey, is
not based upon anything authentic but that
they were largely the creatures of his pro-
lific brain, and that many of them were
manufactured to enable him to extend the
list to such proportions that they might be
made sufficient argumentation as to form
the basis of his book which he desired to sell
upon the market.[8]

Anyone who has seriously studied the history of
Freemasonry recognizes the problem of fraudulent documents that were put together in order to create a paper
trail for Freemasonry that goes beyond the establishment of the London Lodge in 1717.

It was the age in which "antiquity" was viewed as
the basis of validity. Various Protestant churches such
as the Church of England sought to demonstrate that
their origins go all the way back to the first century
instead of the Reformation. Cardinal Newman and the
Oxford Movement grew out of this "antiquity" fad.

Thus it was not strange that the validity of Freemasonry was thought by Masonic apologists to depend
entirely on its antiquity. But since no such antiquity
existed, it had to be invented for the good of the Craft.
The end was thought to justify the means in this case.

The old manuscripts and charters which formed
the basis of Freemasonry's claim to antiquity are for the
most part frauds. Historians have chipped away at them
one by one. These fraudulent documents have come
from both England and the United States and have
misled many Masons as to their own history.

The Antiquity Manuscript

Dr. Mackey points put that the Masonic words were
inserted into the Antiquity Manuscript by Preston

when he put it into his *Illustrations*. The Antiquity Manuscript, which supposedly "proved" that Freemasonry existed before 1717, was later quoted by Hughan as genuine. But an original of this manuscript has been found which reveals the "criminal inaccuracy" of Preston.[9]

The Leland/Locke Manuscript

The Leland Manuscript was supposedly written by King Henry VI. It first appeared in the "Gentleman's Magazine" along with a letter of introduction supposedly from the famous philosopher John Locke.

It was picked up and quoted by Huddesford, *The Pocket Companion*, Calcott's *Candid Disquistion*, Hutchinson, Dermott's *Ahiman Rezon*, Preston's *Illustrations*, Noorthouck's *Constitution*, and has even surfaced in a French translation through Thory and in German through Lessing, Krause, and several others. It is still being quoted as proof of the Craft's antiquity.[10]

A. E. Waite calls it "a peculiarly clumsy forgery" produced in the middle of the eighteenth century.[11] Mackey agreed with Gould that it was "an impudent forgery."[12] The letter by Locke is a forgery as well.[13]

The John Moore 1715 Letter

Horace Smith of Philadelphia claimed to have a letter written in 1715 by John Moore in which he stated that he had "spent a few evenings in festivity with my Masonic brothers."

Hughan, Stillson, Newton, and others accepted Smith's claim without ever asking to see the letter. When Smith was finally challenged to produce the letter, it began to be apparent to all that this letter never existed.[14]

The Henry Bell 1754 Letter

Melvin Johnson comments,

> It is now admitted by every Masonic student, both within and without Pennsylvania, that there never was such a letter. The story is like that about the Rhode Island document of 1656 or 1658 and the John Moore letter of 1715. No one of them deserves more dignified reference than to call it a "fake" pure and simple.[15]

The Charter of Cologne

Sometimes the forgery is discovered by the kind of paper on which it is written. The Charter of Cologne which claims to have been written in 1535 is written on paper manufactured in the late seventeenth or early eighteenth century according to the University of Leyden.[16]

The fact that it is quoted as genuine by Oliver, Krause, Findel, and a host of others cannot erase the physical evidence. Both Mackey and Gould are forced to label it "apocryphal."[17]

Any list of fraudulent Masonic documents must also include the Steinmetz Catechism, the Chapter of York, the Charter of Larmenius or Transmission, the Latin Constitution of the Scottish Rite, and the Malcolm Canmore Charter.[18]

Commenting on the attempt to establish the antiquity of Freemasonry upon "old" manuscripts whose validity is in question, Darrah points out that there is absolutely no proof of the genuineness of these documents and in some instances reliable critics have declared them to be forgeries [19]

We can understand the desperate need of those Masonic writers who wanted to claim that their Lodge was the "first" or the "oldest" Lodge in their nation or state. But to conspire to deceive their fellow Masons by creating false documents can never be justified.

The Fifth Principle

Anti-Masonic writers have generally been as unreliable as Masonic apologists. In their zeal to attack Freemasonry, they have been willing to use fantasy, fraud, and deceit. They have even created bogus documents when needed. Their writings must not be taken at face value.

Most anti-Masonic writers are far too gullible in believing the extravagant claims of overzealous, misinformed, or devious Masonic writers who have not done Freemasonry a favor by making outlandish statements which provided much fodder for the guns of the anti-Masons.

Too many Masonic writers have arrogantly claimed that they speak for the whole Craft when they give their personal interpretation of the origin and symbols of Freemasonry.

In one sense, the anti-Masons are victims of those Masonic writers who state that there is a "secret teaching" in Freemasonry which is revealed only to a chosen few in the order. It does not occur to the anti-Mason that if this were true, why are these writers revealing such "secrets" in their books? And why do all such writers contradict each other?

Since there are as many "secrets" as there are writers, if there were dark "secrets" in Freemasonry which were veiled by some kind of conspiracy, there would have been a uniform exposure of them down through the years. But when you have hundreds of

Masonic writers who all claim that their personal views of Freemasonry are the hidden "secret teachings" of the Craft, either one of them is telling the truth and the rest are liars or they are all liars. But they cannot all be telling the truth.

Another error typically made by anti-Masons is the assumption that Freemasonry is based on the writings of a single individual. They usually pick Albert Pike as the official "spokesman" of Freemasonry.

Although it clearly violates the Landmarks of Masonry to adopt the religious views of one man as "the" view of the Craft, some Masons have said that Albert Pike speaks for the whole Craft. Thus anti-Masons can hardly be faulted for using the strange beliefs of Albert Pike to attack Masonry. We will deal with Pike later on in our study.

Two notable anti-Masonic frauds deserve special notice.

The Norton Affair

An orthodox Jew by the name of Jacob Norton petitioned the Grand Lodge of Massachusetts to remove the obvious Christian elements in Freemasonry such as references to St. John, the cross, the Crusades, etc.

The Grand Lodge naturally refused to alter anything in the Rite. In great bitterness, Norton resigned from the Craft and attacked it by making false and misleading statements concerning the history of the Lodge and its teachings.

The amazing thing is that Norton's misinformation was accepted as genuine by subsequent Masonic writers such as Rollins, Hughan, and Gould. They did not know that they were basing their work on the writings of an anti-Mason![20] They were basing their conclusions on Norton's fantasies.

The Luciferian Conspiracy

Of all the attacks against the Craft, none is so vicious as the charge that Masons are a secret cult of devil worshipers or satanists and that at some point in the higher degrees they must pass through a Luciferian initiation. When most Masons hear of a "Luciferian conspiracy" in Freemasonry, they simple shrug it off in the belief that no one would seriously entertain such a scurrilous charge.

Since most Masons in the United States are members of Christian churches and many clergymen belong to the Fraternity, the idea that they are all involved in some kind of devil cult is absurd. Can anyone seriously think that such thirty-third degree Masons as Senator Jesse Helms, the Christian champion of conservative politics, is a worshiper of Lucifer? Or that one of the most well-known evangelists in the world is a Luciferian because he is a thirty-third degree Mason? It would be helpful to pause and consider the origin of the Luciferian charge.

One of the most interesting episodes in the history of Freemasonry is the anti-Masonry movement spawned in nineteenth-century France by one Leo Taxil.[21] What is known about Taxil does not endear him to the bosom of anyone. He was thrown out of a Catholic seminary before he took holy orders. Although the exact cause for his expulsion is not known, the result is. As a reaction, he became a raving atheist, an anti-Catholic and anticleric. He spent his time printing scandalous stories of the sexual crimes of priests, monks, and nuns. He was quite adept at making up stories when needed.

He joined the Masonic Lodge as another way to thumb his nose at the clergy. He was welcomed at first because French Masonry has always been infected with skeptics, anticlerics, and revolutionaries. But not long after, Taxil's lies and fabrications caused him to be thrown out of the Lodge. He now became as zealous an anti-Mason as he was an anti-Catholic.

According to his own testimony, it was at this time that he came up with a brilliant idea that would enable him to take vengeance on Freemasonry and Catholicism at the same time!

First, he would feign re-conversion to Catholicism. This he attributed to a vision of Joan of Arc. He renounced his former works as lies and was received back into the Church.

Second, he would whip the clergy into a frenzy against Masonry by "revealing" that it was actually a secret Luciferian devil cult. He could count on the gullibility of the clergy to believe even the wildest stories. His revenge against the Masons would be complete as the Pope issued his bulls against it.

Third, he would launch his attack on Masonry by inventing whatever documents he needed. He even invented a Luciferian speech which he attributed to Albert Pike whom he claimed was the supreme ruler of all Masons. More on this fraud later.

Fourth, he would finally reveal to the world that the whole thing from beginning to end was a fraud. This in turn would reveal the gullibility of the clergy and embarrass the church. Not only would Masonry be destroyed but the church would be held up to ridicule.

In 1886, Taxil wrote *Les Soeurs Maconnes*, the first of several books in which he "revealed" the secret sexual and satanic rites connected with adoptive Masonry for women. All of Europe was soon filled with his wild stories of satanic orgies in the secret chambers of the Lodge. Just as he planned, the clergy were whipped into a frenzy and the Pope did issue his bulls. The Catholic Church in Europe started a vast anti-Masonic movement that shook Freemasonry to its core.

Taxil's charge of Luciferianism and Pike's implication in it was picked up by Charles Hacks in 1892 and together they published a series of booklets under the title of *Le Diable Au Dix-Neuvieme Siecle*. The charge was later repeated in *La Femme et L'Enfant Dans La Franc-Maconnerie Universelle* by Abel De La Rive.

When we examined this book, we found that the only authority cited (p. 590) to prove that Albert Pike said among other things, "Yes, Lucifer is God" (p. 588) was Taxil's work, *Rituel du Palladium Nouveau et Reforme*!

Even though Taxil admitted that Pike's Luciferian sermon was a complete hoax, in recent times it reappeared in an English translation by Lady Queensborough in *Occult Theosophy* (1931).

With Queensborough as his source, it was later picked up and used in 1977 by Dave Johnson.[22] It has since made its way throughout the anti-Masonic literature of the 1980s: Harmon R. Taylor,[23] Eustace Mullins,[24] Ed Decker,[25] Jack Harris,[26] William Schnoebelen/James Spencer,[27] Sheldon Emry[28], and Jim Shaw/Tom McKinney.[29]

While Taxil's hoax must be rejected for the lie that it was, this is not to say that there has never been Masons who were Luciferians, devil worshippers, or worse. That there has been and are now Masonic authors who are "Luciferian" cannot be denied. There are some New Age Masonic writers such as A. E. Waite, Hall, etc. who would have to be labeled as Luciferians.

The Sixth Principle

The most significant error that is frequently made in discussions of the history of Freemasonry is the assumption that present-day Freemasonry can be traced back to a single origin. This is called the fallacy of reductionism in logic.

When you look upon a great river as it flows into the sea, it would be absurd to imagine that all the water in that river came from a single source. No, as it made its way through the countryside, countless run-offs, creeks, streams, tributaries, and rivers contributed their water to make that river what it was.

In the same way, Freemasonry is a living river which has had countless sources for its symbols, rites, and teachings. To pretend that what we call Freemasonry today is the product of a single origin is impossible. Too many influences, too many movements, and too many leaders have come and gone.

For example, while it would be erroneous to say that present-day Masonry came from Rosicrucianism as a single origin, it would be perfectly proper to say that Rosicrucianism had a clear influence on French Masonry and its symbols and teachings can still be found in some of the higher degrees.

The same can be said of Swedenborgianism. While its influence on Swedish Masonry cannot be denied and its influence can still be seen in some of the higher degrees, it would be wrong to say that Swedenborgianism is *the* origin of present-day Freemasonry.

It became clear to us after reading hundreds of Masonic books, lectures, and articles that the attempt to trace present-day Freemasonry to a single origin is impossible, because, like a living language, Freemasonry is always evolving and changing as new influences bear upon it.

Conclusion

The study of Freemasonry is a deep subject, and it requires special care due to all the fraudulent claims made by Masons and non-Masons alike. But these six principles will keep us safe as we strive after the truth of the origins, history, and teachings of Freemasonry.

2

CHRISTIAN ORIGINS

It may come as a surprise to many Masons to discover that, from the very beginning, Freemasonry was viewed as a Christian institution and its symbols, degrees, and ceremonies were all interpreted according to fundamental Christian doctrines.

The founders of Masonry did not view themselves as pagans, cultists, occultists, Mayans, druids, witches, Hindus, or Buddhists. They never claimed that Masonry descended from ancient mystery cults or the worship of Isis. They knew nothing of such ideas.

The Christian interpretation of Freemasonry was the accepted norm until the later half of the nineteenth century. All of the early writers were committed Christians and many of them were clergymen of conservative churches. A Christian view of the origin of the Lodge was given by Anderson, Hutchinson, Oliver, Webb, Lyon, Hughan, and many others.

Hutchinson gave a distinctively evangelical interpretation of Masonry. He interpreted the third degree as referring to Jesus Christ in the following words.

The great Father of All, commiserating the miseries of the world, sent His only Son, who was innocence itself, to teach the doctrine of salvation, by whom man was raised from the death of sin unto the life of righteousness; from the tomb of corruption unto the chambers of hope; from the darkness of despair to the celestial beams of faith.

Thus the Master Mason represents a man under the Christian doctrine saved from the grave of iniquity and raised to the faith of salvation. As the great testimonial that we are risen from the state of corruption, we bear the emblem of the Holy Trinity as the insignia of our vows and of the origin of the Master's order.[1]

Mackey comments,

The christianization of the third or Master's degree, that is, the interpretation of its symbols as referring to Christ and to Christian dogmas, is not peculiar to nor original with Hutchinson. It was the accepted doctrine of almost all his contemporaries, and several of the rituals of the eighteenth century contain unmistakable traces of it.

Even as late as the middle of the nineteenth century, Dr. Oliver had explicitly declared that if he had not been fully convinced that Freemasonry is a system of Christian ethics—that it contributes its aid to point the way to the Grand Lodge above, through the Cross of Christ—he should never have been found among the number of its advocates. The interpretation of the symbols of Freemasonry from a Christian point of view was, therefore, at the period when Hutchinson advanced his theory, neither novel to the Craft nor peculiar to him.[2]

The position of Dr. Oliver is clear,

> The conclusion is therefore obvious. If the lectures of Freemasonry refer only to events which preceded the advent of Christ, and if those events which consist exclusively of admitted types of the Great Deliverer, who was preordained to become a voluntary sacrifice for the salvation of mankind, it will clearly follow that the Order was originally instituted in accordance with the true principles of the Christian religion.[3]

According to Mackey, the first attempt to de-Christianize the Craft was by Hemming in 1813.[4]

The Fraternity rejected Hemming's attempt to de-Christianize the Craft. The Norton affair already alluded to in chapter one is another example of the Christian nature of early Masonry. Indeed, it was not until after the anti-Masonic movement from 1826–1836, when conservative Christians were forced out of Freemasonry, that the twin process of de-Christianizing and paganizing the Craft could get underway.

Due to the anti-Masonic hysteria of the period following the murder of Captain Morgan by some misguided Masons, such church leaders as Charles Finney, D. L. Moody, Charles Blanchard, Alexander Campbell, and R. A. Torrey managed to pull nearly all of the evangelical Christians out of Freemasonry.

Many conservative churches told their Masonic members that they had to quit Masonry or get out of the church. Families and churches were torn into pieces as the controversy raged from one end of the country to the other.

With this kind of pressure, the churches were able to shut down over half of the Lodges in the country. They even managed to shut down every single Lodge in the state of Vermont! The Christian majority of the Lodge was forced to leave the Craft.

As the conservative Christians left Freemasonry, they handed it over to those members who did not care what the Christian church or its leaders had to say. The vast majority of the Masons who took over leadership positions after the anti-Masonic purges were not Christians and began to reinterpret the Craft according to anti-Christian principles.

Albert Pike stated that, "The best friends of Masonry in America were the anti-Masons of 1826" because they "purified Masonry by persecution."[5] According to Pike, the anti-Masonic movement drove the Christian majority out of the Lodge and this left the way clear for him to redesign the entire Craft according to his own pagan religious views. The nature of those views will be examined in some detail later.

Pike expressed nothing but contempt for the historic Christian interpreters of Freemasonry,[6] and singled out Webb and Preston for special ridicule.[7] Lest anyone think that he did not understand the historic Christian view of Masonry, he described it in great detail and then dismissed it with a wave of his hand.[8]

As we commenced our research, we decided to read all the Masonic literature in its chronological order beginning with Anderson's *Constitutions* written in 1723. This procedure made it crystal clear that Freemasonry was understood to be a Christian institution until the anti-Masonic movement of 1826.

Starting in 1871, Pike tried but failed to shake Masonry free from its Christian heritage. His pagan views were ignored for the most part in his own day. The attempt to paganize the Craft did not really get under way until the 1920s when there was an avalanche of Masonic books which sought to trace Masonry to pagan origins. But we must emphasize that the pagan interpretation of the Craft was by and large limited to the leadership. Pike's book, *Morals and Dogmas*, is so poorly written that very few Masons own a copy of it. Or, if they do, it is hard to imagine that they have ever read more than two or three pages of it.

During the same 1920s, when the leadership was becoming pagan in its views of the Craft, millions of conservative Christians flooded back into Freemasonry. One example would be the hundreds of thousands of conservative Southern Baptists who joined the Fraternity. It was during this time that the Craft recorded its highest growth in membership in its history.

Since many of these new members were pastors, elders, and deacons in their churches, they naturally picked up the original Christian interpretation of the symbols and rites of Freemasonry. Thus while the leadership was becoming pagan, the bulk of the membership returned to the original Christian view.

Since the 1920s, Freemasonry has developed along two different tracks. For the vast majority, the Craft is a fraternity and not a religion. In particular, it is not some kind of pagan religion which would contradict Christian convictions. This is why many members feel insulted when a modern anti-Mason calls them druids or witches.

On the other hand, there is a small vocal minority which openly calls Freemasonry a religion and dogmatically states that Masonry is in fact a revival of certain ancient pagan religions which are all openly anti-Christian.

Since they are constantly writing books on Freemasonry which give it a pagan slant and they arrogantly claim to speak for the whole Fraternity, is it any wonder that anti-Masons have a field day with their extreme statements? In many of their books, modern pagan writers such as Manly Hall do not hesitate to castigate the vast Christian majority of the Craft as "stupid" and "ignorant." There is clearly a civil war going on within Freemasonry itself that must be resolved one way or the other.

The tension in the Lodge between the pagans and the Christians has resulted in a tremendous decline in attendance and membership. This tension is in reality a fight over whose religious convictions will be allowed to interpret the symbols and rites of the Craft. For example, does the Masonic triangle still represent the Christian Trinity of The Father, Son, and Holy Spirit as the founders of Freemasonry believed, or does it now represent the Hindu trinity of Krishna, Shiva, and Brahma as claimed by the modern pagan writers? It is obvious to anyone that the conflict is irrefutably religious in nature.

The persistence of the Christian interpretation explains why millions of sincere Christians presently belong to the Craft and do not see any conflict between it and their Christian convictions. They do not believe in the new pagan interpretation of Freemasonry and continue to believe in the historic Christian interpretation of the Craft. They represent the "silent" majority of Freemasonry.

Since we will examine this issue in greater detail later on in the book, let us now return to the task at hand and survey the early Christian ideas of the origins of Freemasonry.

Prebiblical Origins

Early Masons such as Anderson, Hutchinson, and Oliver attempted to give Freemasonry an aura of antiquity by tracing its beginnings to prebiblical times.

Since the symbols of Freemasonry illustrate God's

plan of salvation through the saving work of Jesus Christ, Freemasonry began in the eternal decrees of God before the foundation of the world.

They held that Freemasonry was also a part of the original religion of all humanity which God revealed to Adam in the Garden. It was a monotheistic religion which reflected the values and truths later revealed in Scripture. This is why the first Landmark is to believe in only one God.

Pagan religions are a corruption of this original religion. Paganism with its many gods is thus a falling away from the monotheistic biblical religion and from Freemasonry which was part of that religion.

It was in this sense that the Anglican clergyman Anderson said that Freemasonry is the "ancient" religion to which all people agree. He was not referring to some foreign pagan religion but the original biblical religion revealed at the dawn of history.

Biblical Origins

Anderson, Hutchinson, Oliver, and the other early writers did not claim that Buddha was the first Mason as Pike did,[9] but referred to the following biblical characters as being the first members of the Craft.

Adam	The Patriarchs
Cain	Joseph
Abel	Moses
Seth	Solomon and the
Lamech and sons	builders of the
Tubal-Cain	Temple
Nimrod	John the Baptist
Noah and his sons	Jesus
The builders of	St. John and
the Tower of	St. Andrew
Babel	King Herod

Postbiblical Origins

Some early writers also traced the origin of Freemasonry to John the Baptist, the beginning of the Christian church when the ancient true religion was restored. Others referred to the Crusades or to certain pre-Reformation movements which sought to return to the pure Christian faith.

Criticisms

The attempt to find the origins of Freemasonry in a prebiblical religion or in the Bible itself is an exercise in futility. There is absolutely nothing in the Bible about Freemasonry. To say that Adam's fig leaf was a Masonic apron stretches all credulity.

Masons have traditionally been told that the Craft began with the building of Solomon's Temple. But there is nothing in the biblical record that even remotely hints at this idea.

Masons have also been told that the legend of Hiram Abiff which plays an important role in the third degree, is a part of the biblical record. In truth, the legend of Hiram Abiff has nothing to do with the Bible. The legend is nowhere recorded in Scripture. We are not told where, how, or by whom Hiram died. As a matter of fact, the Masonic legend combines several different individuals in the Bible called Hiram or Hirum into one composite individual. The legend has no basis in fact.

Conclusion

While we cannot accept these early theories of where Masonry began, it does reveal that for nearly two centuries, the Craft was viewed as a Christian institution completely compatible with biblical religion. The idea that Freemasonry came from pagan origins never crossed its early members' minds.

3

THE LEGACY OF ALBERT PIKE

No discussion of Freemasonry is complete without dealing with the significance of Albert Pike. His contribution to modern Scottish Rite Freemasonry is so important that the Supreme Council went on record stating,

> It would be impossible to overestimate the importance of Grand Commander Albert Pike's more than 30 years of work for Scottish Rite. Of primary importance, he edited our Rituals of the Degrees and compiled *Morals and Dogma*.[1]

His Importance

Those Masonic writers who agreed with his attempt to de-Christianize and then paganize the Lodge have never ceased to refer to Pike as the greatest Mason who ever lived.

In 1919, *The Masonic Text Book* referred to Pike as,

> One of the most illustrious Masons in all the ages, and who was an acknowledged authority upon all Masonic questions.[2]

In 1925, Carl Claudy called Pike, "Greatest of the Masons as he was greatest of mystics."[3]

In 1970, the occultist A. E. Waite did not hesitate to call Pike, "a master genius of Masonry." He goes on to say,

> He raised the *Scottish Rite* from a comparatively obscure position, encompassed by many competitors, to its present unrivaled state as a High-Grade system of Masonry. Dr. Fort Newton has said in his picturesque manner that Pike found Masonry in a log cabin and left it in a temple.
> ... Pike rewrote its Rituals and managed its affairs for a long period with conspicuous success... his name will be ever green and of precious memory in all American Masonry.[4]

We could fill several pages with Masonic writers who praised Pike as the most important influence on American Masonry. And anyone who has ever read modern Masonic literature has run across the dozens of passages where it is claimed that Pike is *the* spokesman for the Craft.

As you enter the House of the Temple in Washington, D.C., which is the headquarters of the Supreme Council of the Scottish Rite of Freemasonry, you will encounter a life-size bust of Albert Pike. It marks the place where he is now buried by a special act of Congress.

You then proceed to "The Albert Pike Room" where

his unpublished works and other artifacts are on display. Pike's personal library is also housed at the Temple. After your Temple visit, you can see a life-size statue of Pike near the corner of Third and Indiana Ave., N.W.

Obviously, not just anyone gets buried by an act of Congress, has a temple reared in his honor, and has his statue placed in the nation's capital. Why was this man so honored? What was he like? What was his background?

Few Resources

Biographical resources for the life of Albert Pike are few. He is not listed in standard encyclopedias and he does not even appear in any of the biographical dictionaries. The only published biography of Pike's life was written by Fred Allsopp in 1928. But it is too general and fails to reveal the details of his background or life.[5]

In 1909, The Supreme Council issued a small booklet on Pike entitled *Albert Pike, Centenary Souvenir of His Birth, 1809–1909*. In it we are told that Albert Pike was born in 1809, the same year of birth as William Gladstone, Abraham Lincoln, Oliver Wendell Holmes, Charles Darwin, and Edgar Allen Poe. But because it is a "souvenir" of his birth, the bulk of this booklet is composed of statements about Pike's greatness and reveals very little about his life or times.

William Boyden issued his *Bibliography of the Writings of Albert Pike* in 1921. He evidently published it himself as no publisher was listed. It was a catalogue of all the published and unpublished books, manuscripts, lectures, articles, letters, and poems of Pike. But no biographical information was given.

The Supreme Council in 1986 issued another booklet on Pike, but it is just 40 pages long and only a distillation of seven "sermons" on the greatness of Pike. It did not give us much information.

Since we wanted more information on Pike, we received permission from the House of the Temple in Washington, D.C., to examine all of Pike's unpublished manuscripts, lectures, poems, and letters.

The Head Librarian of the Temple was one of the most gracious people we have ever met. She gave us complete access to all the unpublished documents in the Albert Pike Room, the Temple Library, and the letter files.

Imagine our surprise when we found that Pike had begun to write his own biography before he died. This unpublished manuscript yielded much helpful information. In his own words, Pike described how he had the honor of meeting such famous and powerful men as General Lafayette, Davy Crockett, Daniel Webster, Henry Clay, Sam Houston, and Zachary Taylor. According to Pike, he moved in the highest circles of politics and finance and had access to the White House and Congress both before and after the Civil War. His autobiography revealed many details about his life which are not recorded anywhere else. For example, he complained that he had forgotten how to translate Latin, Greek, and Hebrew.

While we were reading our way through all the manuscripts in the Albert Pike Room, we finally found a biography that does justice to the life of Albert Pike. In 1955, Walter Lee Brown submitted a four-volume doctoral dissertation on the life of Albert Pike to the University of Texas. This unpublished dissertation is without a doubt the definitive biography of Albert Pike. Why it has never been published remains a mystery.

During Brown's research, he found that Pike had been raised in a very devout Christian home. His father was known for being both pious and active in church work. Both Albert and his father faithfully sang in the choir of the Episcopal church (I:6).

Brown also reveals that Pike was not the linguist many have claimed. For example, Albert Pike did not know Sanskrit and could not translate the Vedas if his life depended on it. Pike openly admitted that he used the Vedic translations of Müller, Müir, Wilson, Bleeck, and Haug (IV:841).

By 1874, Pike had written over 12,000 pages on the Vedas (IV:842). This so exhausted him that he never again did any serious study or writing (IV:843-844). By 1887, it was obvious that Pike had become a recluse and rarely went outside of his house (IV:862).

His Life

According to the above sources, Albert Pike was born on December 29, 1809 in Boston, Massachusetts. His father was a simple shoemaker. When he was four years old, his family moved to Newburyport, Massachusetts. This small city was one of the centers of the Great Awakening under Jonathan Edwards and the final resting place of the great evangelist, George Whitefield.

He was born into a pious Christian home and faithfully attended his father's Episcopal church. As a student, Pike showed remarkable intelligence and was accepted at Harvard. But due to his father's death and the financial ruin it brought upon the family, Pike left Harvard.

In 1831, Pike headed West traveling mostly by foot due to a lack of money. He ended up in St. Louis where he joined a group of trappers going into hostile Indian territory. As a fur trapper, Pike wandered around Texas, New Mexico, and even into Mexico itself.

In November of 1832, failing to make his fortune as a trapper, Pike decided to head down to New Orleans. But he got confused in his directions and went north instead of south and found himself in Fort Smith, Arkansas. He taught school there for a few months until he moved to Little Rock in October of 1833.

In Little Rock, Pike became the editor of a newspaper called *The Arkansas Advocate*. In 1834, although he had never had any schooling in the subject beyond his own reading, Pike applied for a license to practice law. This was granted as most "lawyers" in those days never went to law school.

It was in Little Rock that Pike applied for admission to the Western Star Lodge in 1850. He soon worked his way up through the degrees granted by Templar Masonry.

At the beginning of 1853, Pike moved to New Orleans where he encountered the Scottish Rite for the first time. He had not even heard of it up to this point.

Pike joined the Scottish Rite, became friends with Albert Mackey, and was granted the fourth to the thirty-second degree by Mackey himself in Charleston, South Carolina. He did not receive the thirty-third degree until 1857. He joined the Supreme Council the following year. In 1859, Pike became the Grand Commander of the Supreme Council and held that office until his death in 1891.

Although a Yankee by birth, during the Civil War he became a Confederate soldier by choice. He came to this position not only by his residence but also by his low views of blacks.

His war record is not impressive. He did not hesitate to disobey his superior officers and, depending on whether you believe the Army or Pike, he was either relieved of his duties or he resigned.

President Lincoln did not grant him amnesty after the war and all his possessions were confiscated. Pike fled to Canada in order to escape further punishment. Lincoln was not a Mason and Pike had to run literally for his life.

In 1865, when Andrew Johnson became President, since he was a Mason, Pike applied for and received his amnesty papers and went to Memphis where he called for the Scottish Rite to resume its work.

It was during this crucial period of reorganization after the war that Pike rewrote the degrees from the fourth to the thirty-third. No one opposed him and he had a free hand to de-Christianize and then paganize the higher degrees.

In 1877, Pike was named the Provincial Grand Master by the Grand Lodge in Edinburgh, Scotland. He was now the undisputed head of American Scottish Rite Masonry and his word was law. For example, when in March of 1891 he was told that he was going to die, he personally chose who would succeed him as Grand Commander.

After his death on April 2, 1891, Pike had two funerals: one according to the Masonic rites and the other according to the Episcopal rites.

One would hope that maybe in death he had finally returned to his father's church. But he was later dug up and reburied at the House of the Temple. It was only appropriate that his remains should be removed from a Christian burial site as he hated the Christian church and everything for which it stood.

His Writings

The first literary works of Albert Pike were poems or hymns which he devoted to the worship of various pagan Greek and Roman gods and goddesses such as Athena or Diana of Ephesus. He later added Eastern deities. Some of them go as far back as 1829 when he was 20 years old.

It was probably while Pike was at Harvard that his faith in Christianity was destroyed by skeptical professors. They then pointed him to the pagan religions of the East as the place where truth could be found.

During the early part of the nineteenth century, in both England and in the United States, a fascination for anything Eastern had sprung up as British soldiers returned from India with amazing stories of Hindu gurus and their teachings. It became quite a fad to become a Hindu.

It was also during this period that the sacred writings of Hinduism, the Vedas, were first translated into English and were now accessible to those who wanted to try a religion other than Christianity.

In 1836, while in Little Rock, Pike published some of these poems in a book under the alias of Sam Bannacle which he entitled, *The Lays of the Humburger*. They were republished in 1899 after his death as *Hymns to the Gods*, and then yet again by Allsopp in 1916.

Pike did write a few secular and love poems as well as hymns to the gods. One particularly striking poem was written after his wife died.

In 1858, Pike delivered a lecture entitled "The Meaning of Freemasonry." What is interesting is that nowhere in this lecture did Pike refer to pagan mystery cults, the Kabbalah, or the Vedas as having anything to do with the origin of Freemasonry. He stated,

> I will not claim that it was coeval with Noah or with Enoch, or that its Lodges were held within the holy walls of the first Temple in Jerusalem, or even that it arose during the times of the Crusades. It is enough to say that its origin is hidden in the mists and shadows of antiquity.[6]

When you compare this 1858 lecture with Pike's *Morals and Dogmas*, written in 1871, it is obvious that he went through a dramatic change in his views of Freemasonry. What could have produced such a remarkable change in his views?

First, the suffering and death connected with the Civil War had a profound effect on Pike according to his own testimony. In his autobiography, he relates that it was during this period that he lost not only his wife but also most of his children. In his grief, he said,

> I have had ten children, but I have only three left now. Since the war, I have been studying the Vedas trying to find out the meaning of it (p. 74).

Throughout his life, Pike would suffer spells of severe depression. At times, he would become a recluse—not seeing anyone, not going anywhere. It was during these dark periods in his life that he meditated on the Hindu Vedas and changed the course of American Scottish Rite Freemasonry.

The French Connection

In addition to the Vedas, Pike undertook a major study of French Masonry which he later made into a huge unpublished manuscript called *Materials for the History of Freemasonry in France and Elsewhere on the Continent of Europe from 1718–1859*. It is a massive work of six volumes containing 1460 pages.

In this manuscript, Pike reveals that he used the French Lodge as his guide in redesigning the fourth to the thirty-third degrees in the Scottish Rite.

This insight is the "key" to Albert Pike. This explains why his writings became increasingly radical, anti-Christian, and occultic. These elements have been a part of French Masonry from the beginning and eventually led the Grand Lodge in London to sever all Masonic relationships to the French Lodge.

It would seem to the objective observer that the

very things which the London Lodge repudiated, Pike turned around and used to remold the Scottish Rite!

Pike's French studies also led him to embrace the occult writings of a Kabbalist who called himself Eliphas Levi. The real name of Eliphas Levi was Alphonse Louis Constant who was born in Paris in 1810. He was thrown out of a Catholic seminary and denied the priesthood because of his involvement in the occult and magic.

In 1855, he wrote *The Doctrine and Ritual of Magic, The History of Magic* in 1860, and *The Key of the Mysteries* in 1861. He was the most influential magician of the nineteenth century. He was a Mason as well as a member of a secret occult society started in England by Bulmer Lytton. But after he published some of their secrets, they expelled him.

Levi built upon the idea which the Masonic writer Higgins had first given in his book, *Anacalypsis*, in 1835. Pike was familiar with this book as well and it played a part in his thinking. Higgins agreed with the Masonic founders that there was one ancient religion which all people accepted at the dawn of history and that Freemasonry was part of this "ancient" faith. But he then turned their position upside down and claimed this original religion was pagan in nature and not at all biblical. Biblical religions such as Christianity were corruptions of the original faith. The true "old-time religion" was closer to Hinduism and the ancient mystery cults. Eliphas Levi added to the Higgins thesis by claiming that the Jewish Kabbalah also reflected the "ancient" religion of all mankind.

Anyone familiar with the writings of Eliphas Levi recognizes that Pike plagiarized much of Levi's writings. That this is true can be demonstrated by the following example. The following passage is from Levi's writings.

Behind the veil of all the hieratic and mystical allegories of ancient doctrines, behind the darkness and strange ordeals of all in initiations, under the seal of all sacred writings, in the ruins of old Nineveh or Thebes, on the crumbling stones of old temples and on the blackened visage of the Assyrian or Egyptian sphinx, in the monstrous or marvelous paintings which interpret to the faithful of India the inspired pages of the Vedas, in the cryptic emblems of our old books on alchemy, in the ceremonies practiced at reception by all secret societies, there are found indications of a doctrine which is everywhere the same and everywhere concealed.[7]

Now, compare what Levi wrote with what Pike wrote in his *Morals and Dogma* (p. 729).

Through the veil of all the hieratic and mystic allegories of ancient dogmas, under the seal of all the scared writings, in the ruins of Nineveh or Thebes, on the worn stones of the ancient temples, and on the blackened face of the sphinx of Assyria or Egypt, in the monstrous or marvelous pictures which the sacred pages of the Vedas translate for the believers of India, in the strange emblems of our old books of alchemy, in the ceremonies of reception practiced by all the mysterious Societies, we find traces of doctrine, everywhere the same, and everywhere carefully hidden.

Most of Pike's intricate Kabbalistic reasoning and the historical material is lifted right out of Levi's works.

A. E. Waite, who wrote *A New Encyclopedia on Free-masonry*, comments,

> There is also his *Morals and Dogma*, an undigested compilation from a great number of sources, in which of his own will and intent he has made it impossible to distinguish between that which is his therein and that which has been "lifted" from the works of others by literal translation and so forth. It comes about in this manner—to cite but one instance—that the brilliant, if shallow, *philosophia occulta* of Eliphas Levi is foisted on the unwary reader as if it were his own, and it occupies scores of pages, scattered there and here.[8]

Waite is in a position to know as he took over the Order of the Golden Dawn, an occult society which gathered around the use of magic and the writings of Eliphas Levi, after Crowley died.[9]

Aleister Crowley, another Mason involved in the occult, was the previous leader of the Golden Dawn. Raised in an evangelical Christian home (Plymouth Brethren), he spent his life rebelling against the Christian faith of his parents and committed "every sin in the book." He called himself "the Beast," painted 666 on his forehead, committed sodomy, and claimed to have sacrificed an infant. Crowley influenced many of the upper class in England and even had the poet Yates under his spell. He claimed to be the living reincarnation of Eliphas Levi.[10]

We wonder if Pike's bouts of depression were caused by his immersion in the occultic writings of French Masonry. He filled his mind with the Kabbalah, which is depressing reading in and of itself. And he dwelt long on the Vedas which are so written as to prevent actually a reader from understanding their meanings.

1871 Publications

Addresses

In 1871, Pike published three works. First, Pike and Mackey published a book together entitled *Addresses*. This book was just a compilation of some of their Masonic lectures.

Masonic Baptism

The Supreme Council next released his second and more controversial book, *Masonic Baptism: Reception of a Louveteau: Adoption*. Most modern-day Masons have never even heard about the rite of Masonic baptism. It was developed by French Masons, but was never a part of English, Scottish, or American Freemasonry.

In the French Lodge, the anticleric radicals had proposed that Freemasonry replace all the sacraments of the Christian church with their own pagan versions of them. They went on to develop Masonic rituals for infant baptism, communion, marriage, confession, and burial. Pike appealed to his American audience to accept Masonic baptism according to "the Acts du Supreme Conseil de France" (p. 5).

He claimed that baptism was originally a pagan rite in such religions as Hinduism, Mithraism, Zoroasterism, the Eleusian Mysteries, Isis worship, etc. It was adopted by the Essenes from pagan sources and later stolen by the Christians who proceeded to corrupt it.

Pike outlined an entire baptismal service with the parents and godparents presenting the boy or girl to be baptized. The Masonic baptismal rite used water, oil, salt, and incense (p. 50). After the Master Mason sprinkled the water on the head of the child, he was to use the oil to make the sign of a triangle on the forehead of the child (p. 53). He then suggested that the godparents place around the neck of the child a necklace with a triangle.

Why did Pike substitute a triangle in the place of the cross?

In *Morals and Dogma* (p. 550), and later in an unpublished manuscript on Masonic symbolism, Pike explained that the triangle referred to the Hindu trinity of Shiva, Krishna, and Brahma. It would appear that Pike deliberately turned the rite of Christian baptism into a Hindu baptismal ceremony!

While American Masons adopted the Masonic ritual for burial, they could not accept all the other Masonic sacraments such as baptism. To have such rituals and then to pretend that Freemasonry is not a religion would be impossible.

Morals and Dogma

The third book of Pike's to come out in 1871 was his famous *Morals and Dogma*. As we have already pointed out, it contains various sections that were lifted out of French occultic writings such as those by Eliphas Levi. It is far too large to give a complete analysis of it in this chapter, but the following summaries of what Pike said might prove interesting to the reader.

On God

Pike believed that the original religion of all people was based upon a belief in the Principle of Eastern Monism as expressed in philosophic Hinduism. Ultimate reality is one and yet two at the same time, like a coin is one and yet has two sides.

This Divine Principle is seen in the duality of good/evil, darkness/light, Yin/Yang, male/female, positive/negative, sun/moon, etc. These dualities were not the Divine Principle but only a manifestation of it. (Little did Pike know that this concept in the twentieth century would become the basis of Rev. Moon's Unification Church.)

For Pike this Principle cannot be described or personalized. To do so is to make false gods. For example, the Bible makes the mistake of personalizing one side of the Principle as evil and the other side as good. It then makes the evil side of the Principle into "Satan" and the good side into "Jehovah."

Thus the biblical God and his counterpoint, the devil, do not really exist. Satan is just God spelled backward according to Pike. As a matter of fact, all the gods of all religions are just so much Baalim. There is the "God," i.e., Divine Principle, beyond, above, and behind all false deities which are but man writ large. The word "God" is just a symbol for the impersonal Principle or Force which underlies all things. There is no personal God, gods, devil, or devils. Thus every religion is false.

Hindus and Buddhists who personalize the Principle into deities and demons are as guilty as the Jews and the Christians. The moment you give the Principle attributes, you have limited it. To limit it is to corrupt it.[11]

On Christianity

Pike claims that the Patriarchs, Joseph, Moses, and Jesus were actually Hindu in belief. Their Hinduism was covered up and corrupted by those who followed them. Their belief in the Divine Principle was taken out of the Bible and it is now hopelessly corrupt. The true teachings of these great men were lost until now.

According to Pike, Christianity is not only false, it is positively evil. The following is a summary of what Pike said about Judaism and Christianity:[12]

> Christianity never taught equality; Christians are hypocrites; Muslims are more trustworthy

than Christians; the churches and the priest-hood govern men by imaginary terrors; Protestants created a mean and miserable God in the imagination of people; the teachers of Christianity are the most ignorant of the true meaning of what they teach; to superimpose the Bible upon Masonic symbols is absurd; Catholicism is despotism and superstition; the early Christians lost the Truth; Christianity came from the Essenes; the Hebrew and Christian God is cruel, bloodthirsty, savage, angry, jealous, revengeful, wavering, irresolute, barbaric, short-sighted, capricious, unjust, vindictive; the Jews are ignorant, narrow-minded, and vindictive with a lower, meaner and more limited idea of God; the New Testament gives only a vulgar faith; Christianity is a religion of Hate and Persecution; the God that Christians worship is just the pagan gods under a new name, a Baalim; the Jews failed to recognize that their Jehovah was only Plato's God called the Demiurge; the God of the Old Testament is the author of evil; the God of the Jews and the Christians is but Man personified, a God of human passions, the God of the Heathen with but a change of name; the Church Fathers were the dunces who led primitive Christianity astray, by substituting faith for science, reverie for experience, the fantastic for the reality, the inquisitors who for so many ages waged against Magism a war of extermination, have succeeded in shrouding in darkness the ancient discoveries of the human mind; so that we now grope in the dark to find again the key of the phenomena of nature; the teachings of the churches are absurd.

Given Pike's blistering attack against the Bible, Judaism, and Christianity, is it any wonder that many Jewish and Christian Masons have left the Lodge? After all, Masonry is not supposed to take sides in religious controversies. The Lodge should not be the place where one's religious convictions are attacked and vilified. Yet, the Jew and the Christian are singled out and ridiculed by Pike.

Pike's attack against Bible-based religions is so vicious that it is no surprise to find that many people consider him an anti-Semitic and anti-Christian bigot. How in the world did the Scottish Rite get drawn into this ugly affair?

Pike's hatred of Christianity grew out of his exposure to French Masonry. That the French Lodge was violently anticleric and anti-Christian is well known. The hatred of French Masons against the church came to full bloom during the French Revolution when they murdered the clergy, raped the nuns, made soup with communion wafers, and installed a naked woman in the Cathedral of Notre Dame and proclaimed her a goddess of reason.[13] This is the source of Pike's bigotry.

Pike was aware that when he denied the existence of the God of the Bible and all other personal gods such as Allah, he was open to the charge of atheism.[14] Practically speaking, Pike was an atheist because he denied the existence of a personal God who stands outside of and independent from the universe. Pantheism is a religious form of atheism.

Pike's Occultic Beliefs

1. Humans are divine and thus we are all gods according to Pike.[15]

2. Truth is relative and cultural. Pike stated, "What is truth to me is not true to another." He goes on to explain truth is a matter of when and where you were born.[16]

3. Ultimate Reality is mind and not matter. What we see with our senses is an illusion. Only "God" really exists.[17]

4. Pike denied the existence of evil: "Evil is merely apparent, and all is in reality good and perfect."[18]

5. Pike believed in the preexistence of the soul in that we came out of "God" and will go back into "God" through reincarnation.[19]

6. Astrology is part of the ancient religion of Freemasonry.[20]

7. Buddha was the first Master Mason.[21]

8. Pike believed in the magic or sorcery that is found in pagan witchcraft and in the occult arts.[22]

Morals and Dogma is nothing more than a presentation of the doctrines of classical Hinduism with a mixture of astrology, magic, and reincarnation.

Instead of being the glory of Pike, *Morals and Dogma* is really his shame. To steal from the literary works of others and to claim it as your own is the exact kind of unethical conduct which is clearly condemned by Masonic ethics.

Pike's Vedic Trilogy

In 1872, Pike finished a manuscript entitled, *Indo-Ayran Deities and Worship as Contained in the Rig-Veda.* This manuscript, which we found in the House of the Temple, summarized some of his studies of the Vedas which are the sacred writings of the Hindus. A small limited edition for Masonic leaders was published in 1930 by the Standard Publishing Company in Louisville, Kentucky.

The material in this book was plagiarized from German scholars such as Max Müller, Martin, Haug, and others. It is an undigested survey of all the ancient gods mentioned in the Rig-Veda. Pike attempted to interpret the hymns to the gods mentioned in the Rig-Veda. Commenting on this Vedic study, Pike claimed in a letter dated 1879,

> The translations of most of the hymns are for the most part nonsense, and their meaning unknown to all the world, as well as to the priests of India, who consider them sacred, as do all European scholars. I am finding out what they mean. I know more about them than anyone else.[23]

It is claimed in the introduction of Pike's *Lectures of the Aryan*, which he finished in 1873, that this was his greatest work. This is the second book in his trilogy of Vedic works. It was published in a limited edition in 1930 by the Standard Publishing Company.

In this work, Pike reveals that he believed in the concept of the "Aryan Master Race"! The German composer Richard Wagner had promoted this idea in his music as far back as 1850. Max Müller, to whom Albert Pike owed so much Vedic material, had popularized this form of racism in his two-volume work, *Lectures on the Science of Language* (London, 1861-1864).

Aryan racism was then championed by Houston Chamberlain, Wagner's son-in-law, in 1899. It was his writings that introduced Adolph Hitler to the concept and led to his attempt to purify the Aryan race by killing off "lower" races such as the Jews. The black race was particularly singled as proof that not all people were created equal.

One is almost tempted to say that Pike's book would have been a bestseller in the Third Reich if it would have been published for the general public instead of for the few members of the Supreme Council.

To put it bluntly, Pike was a racist of the worse sort. Pike's Aryan racism supplies us with the reason why he used the Aryan symbol of the swastika as a Masonic symbol.

Following the racist theories of Max Müller, Pike stated concerning the Aryan race,

> They were white men, as we are, the superior race in intellect, in manliness, the governing race of the world, the conquering race of all other races.[24]

According to Pike, the Aryan race was the original race of mankind. Their religion as found in the Vedas was the original religion and thus, the true one.

The race broke into two groups: The Indo-Aryans who wrote the Rig-Veda and the Irano-Aryans who wrote the Zend-Avesta. Pike comments,

> I have found in both the most profound philosophical and metaphysical ideas, which those of every ancient and modern philosophy and religion have but developed.[25]

In 1874, Pike finished his trilogy on the Vedas with a manuscript entitled *Irano-Aryan Faith and Doctrine as Contained in the Zend-Avesta*. It was published in a limited edition in 1924 by the Standard Publishing Company.

Pike's racism comes to full bloom in this book. He singled out the black race as being the "lowest" race. He claimed that the existence of the blacks proved that both the Creation account of Genesis and Darwin's theory of evolution were false because the white race could not have come from the same source as the black race![26]

Pike's racist views on the black race caused him to say,

> I took my obligation to white men, not
> Negroes. When I have to accept Negroes as
> brethren or leave Freemasonry, I shall leave
> it.[27]

The racist attitudes of the Supreme Commander
Albert Pike prevented the Scottish Rite from accepting
blacks into membership for many, many years. In spite
of all the denials, the facts would indicate that the
Scottish Rite was racist in its attitude toward the black
race. And there are those in Black Freemasonry who
feel that it is still racist to a great degree.

Unpublished Writings

We are not sure as to the dates of some of Pike's
unpublished material. Just when he wrote his *Autobiography* is not stated. Pike's massive six-volume work,
*Materials for the History of Freemasonry in France and
Elsewhere on the Continent of Europe 1718-1859* is not
dated. It proves that he used the French Lodge as his
guide in remolding all the degrees beyond the Blue
Lodge.

Pike's two-volume work entitled *Symbolism* tells
us that,

> It is now certain that there were no degrees
> in Masonry two hundred years ago, and that
> the Master's degree is no more than 150
> years of age (p. 1).

He referred to the Christian interpreters of the
symbolism as "the work of men utterly ignorant of symbolism and are worthless" (p. 3).

Pike's letters sometimes yield a little information
that would not have been known otherwise. For example,
on July 6, 1875, Pike wrote a letter to one of the Brethren in Hawaii in which he stated that he had changed

his mind since writing *Morals and Dogma*, in that he now believed that Freemasonry was indeed a religion because it was the original religion of the Aryans as written in the Vedas.

Conclusion

Pike attempted to remold Scottish Freemasonry into an Aryan religion for the Aryan race complete with its own scriptures, ceremonies, and symbolism. He was deeply involved in occult arts such as magic and astrology as well.

Albert Pike does not deserve the praise that has been heaped upon him since his death. He was not a scholar but a plagiarizer. He was a fraud and a con man to the end. He was a promoter of the same Aryan racism which later led so many millions to their death. What then is the legacy of Albert Pike? *Pike found Freemasonry a Christian institution but left it a Hindu temple.*

4

PAGAN ORIGINS

The attempt of Albert Pike to turn Freemasonry into a pagan temple complete with its own religious ceremonies such as Hindu baptism was a failure during his lifetime. The bulk of the Masons were Christians and they simply refused to be converted to a heathen religion. Pike's Masonic baptismal ritual was seldom used and was eventually abandoned. Indeed, most Masons are not even aware of its existence.

The only ones who immediately followed Pike into paganism were the leaders of the House of the Temple in Washington, D.C. Since that time, they have consistently published only those writers who used pagan religions such as Hinduism to interpret the rituals and symbols of the Craft.

That this is true can be established by many examples. One perfect example would be the writings of Carl Claudy. The Temple published most of his Hinduistic interpretations of the Craft. (See *The Old Past Master; A Master's Wages; Foreign Countries; The Lion's Paw; Introduction to Freemasonry* [3 vols.]; *Masonic*

Harvest; These Were the Brethren, Where Your Treasure Is, etc.)

We could not find a single instance where the Temple published a Christian interpretation of the Lodge. As far as we can determine, all the writers published by The Temple Publishers since Pike have used pagan principles in their books. If they did publish Christian views of the Lodge, our research failed to uncover it.

The Pagan Connection

Since the 1920s, a steady stream of Hinduistic, cultic, and occultic writers have claimed to reveal the "real secrets" of the Craft. The occultist, Manly P. Hall, is but one writer among hundreds who have followed Pike's example in attempting to turn Freemasonry into a Hindu temple.

Because there are so many books which claim that the origin of Freemasonry is to be found in ancient pagan religions, many Masons have fallen victim to the technique that if you repeat a lie often enough, people will begin to believe it.

Too many Masons have been gullible in believing the wildest stories concerning the origin of Freemasonry. They have assumed that the hundreds of pagan writers on the Craft are telling them things which sound scholarship has established.

The same can be said of most anti-Masonic writers. They have accepted as true the most ridiculous stories of when, where, and how Freemasonry began. They too are victims of myths and fables just because they have been repeated over and over again.

We understand that it is more fun to believe that Masonry came from some ancient mystery cult than to accept the fact that it began as a beer party in a London

tavern in 1717. But this does not alter the fact that pagan origin theories must be tested to see if they are *true*. Why should we be content to believe lies about the Craft? Masons above all others should want the truth, the whole truth, and nothing but the truth about the origin of their Craft.

Nothing in Common

The first thing that should make any rational person suspicious of the idea that Freemasonry is an ancient pagan religion from the dawn of time is that all the writers contradict each other as to the time, identity, nature, teachings, and location of this pagan religion.

Masons must ask, "Which pagan religion? Where was it located? What did it teach? When did it appear? Who followed it? How is it the origin of Freemasonry? Can you trace it throughout history in an unbroken line to modern Freemasonry? Do you have any hard evidence to support your claim?"

It would seem that the only thing all writers agree upon is that Freemasonry must not have any Christian elements in it. It must be radically anti-Christian and pagan to the core.

Pagan Claims

One is presented with a chaos of claims by pagan Masonic writers. It would take several hundred pages to go into each claim and refute them one by one. Thankfully, these writers have refuted each other as they put forth their own unique claim.

The following is a summary of the supposed pagan origins of Freemasonry. Most of the writers assumed that the Craft can be traced back to one single pagan origin.

Prehistory Origins

Some have claimed that Freemasonry goes back to "the dawn of time" or to "the very beginning of history." Of course, this automatically means that there is absolutely nothing to back up this claim, making it utterly worthless.

We must also reject as worthless the claim that Freemasonry was the religion of Atlantis or the lost land of Mu. There is not a shred of evidence for such claims, no matter how romantic their nature.

Original Religion

The claim that Freemasonry was the original religion of all people is without foundation. It does not matter if the writer is a Christian or a pagan; no evidence has ever been submitted to support it.

Stonehenge

The claim that the ruins of Stonehenge and all other ruins like it which are scattered around the world are the first Masonic Lodges is a perfect example of a fertile imagination gone wild.

The Occult Arts

Some writers claim that the Craft was the outgrowth of ancient occult arts such as magic, witchcraft, sorcery, astrology, alchemy, and fortunetelling. They point to the magical elements in the higher degrees as proof. Yet, these very elements were put there by French Masons such as Levi who believed in magic. They were not part of the Craft before that time.

Mother India

Others tell us that Freemasonry came from some

ancient religion. But which one? Some say that it must have come from India's Hinduism. But no historical evidence has ever been found for this claim.

Chinese Origins

Others say that China's Buddhism is the source of Freemasonry. But what evidence is there for this claim? None whatsoever.

Egyptian Origins

Many writers deny that Freemasonry started in India or China. They claim it really came from Egypt. But which Egyptian religion?

Some say that it was the worship of Ra. But others say Isis. Or it could have been the cult of Seth or Osirus. But was it the official state religion or one of the mystery cults?

Since no writer offers any evidence as to where, when, or by whom the Craft was started in Egypt and no link is ever shown between it and modern Masonry, their claims must be rejected.

Assyrian Origins

Some Masonic "historians" deny that it was in India, China, or Egypt that the Fraternity began. They claim that it came from the Fertile Crescent of the Middle East. But which religion?

Some say that Freemasonry was a development of Baal worship. Others claim Molochism. No, some claim, it all began with the worship of the sun and the moon. Not so, others claim. The Craft grew out of the Assyrian fertility cults. They go on to interpret all the symbols as phallic symbols. The two pillars, the dot in the circle, the sun and moon, etc., all get a sexual interpretation. But then another writer says it actually came from the Adonis cult.

Palestinian Origins

Some claim that we should look no further than the Holy Land for the origin of Freemasonry. The Druses or the Essenes started the whole thing. But then others say it was actually King Herod who created it. Yet there are those who disagree and instead claim that the Craft began during the Maccabean Wars and was actually a cult of Assassins!

Greek Origins

Leaving behind the mists and shadows of ancient India, China, Egypt, and Assyria, some have claimed that Masonry really began in the religions found in Greece. But which religion?

Some writers say that the Craft was originated by pre-Socratic philosophers such as Pythagoras or Euclid. But there is no indication of this in their writings.

Others claim that the Craft evolved out of the popular myths of the gods and goddesses who lived on Mount Olympus. These writers regale us with all the romantic legends recorded in Greek mythology and take us back to the days of Zeus, Diana, Venus, and Cupid. But, again, there is no evidence to support their theory.

Some writers urge us to reject the idea that the official religion of Greece was the origin of Freemasonry. For the true origin of the Craft, we must look to the great Eleusian mysteries. They usually launch into a tedious description of such "mysteries" but never bother showing the link between them and Masonry.

Other writers object and state that the mystery cults, Mithraism, or Gnosticism are better choices. Others disagree with this and claim that the true origin of Masonry lies in the exalted ideas and rites of the Hermetic Philosophers. But no link between these and modern Masonry is ever established.

Italian Origins

Some writers have given up trying to trace Masonry to ancient times. They are willing to settle for a later date. Instead of India, China, Egypt, Palestine, or Greece, Italy has at times been nominated as the birthplace of the noble Craft.

Freemasonry started in the Roman Colleges according to one theory. Others disagree and claim that it was begun by the Comacines. But then others point to the Gypsies as the ones who started it.

Some writers claim that the Craft first appeared among the Albigenses who hid themselves in the high mountains of Italy. Or, it could have been invented by the heretical Socinians.

French Origins

Other writers claim that the Craft was begun in France by the Rosicrucians. Others say that it was developed by the Jewish mystics who wrote the Kabbalah. But then others point to the Illuminati or to the Theosophists or to the Knights Templar as the origin of Masonry.

Not happy with these choices, some writers claim that it was the French occultists such as Ashmole who invented the whole thing!

Swedish Origins

The occultist Emanuel Swedenborg has been suggested as the one who really created the Craft. But there is no evidence for this idea.

British Origins

Some have claimed that Masonry was begun in Britain by the druids or the builders of Stonehenge. Others claim that it was started by the Culdees. But King Henry VI, Oliver Cromwell, Francis Bacon, the Pretender, and Sir Christopher Wren have also been nominated as the creator of Freemasonry.

American Origins

Turning to the Americas, some Masonic writers have claimed that Freemasonry began among the South American Indians such as the Mayans or the Quiches. Others claim that North American Indians developed Freemasonry as part of their pagan religion.

Conspiracy Theories

In addition to the numerous pagan claims, many writers have suggested that Freemasonry was begun as a plot or a conspiracy.

Some Catholic writers claimed that Freemasonry was a Protestant conspiracy while some Protestants claimed that it was a Catholic conspiracy begun by the Jesuits. But then some Muslim writers say that Freemasonry is an Israeli plot run by Zionist Jews who want to destroy all religions but Judaism.

Still others claim that the Fraternity was invented by the witches or the satanists or Luciferians.

And, lastly, some see the whole thing as the creation of the Rothchilds and other Jewish bankers who use the Craft to control the politics and finance of the world.

We will deal with these themes in a later chapter.

Comments

Obviously, either one Masonic "historian" is right and all the rest are wrong or they are all wrong. But they cannot all be right!

Something is not true just because it is repeated from book to book. The hard cold fact is that Freemasonry did not come from some pagan mystery religion in the ancient world.

Dr. Albert Mackey points out in his *History of Freemasonry* that the attempt to trace the origin of Masonry to the pagan mysteries is "wholly untenable and unsupported by historical evidence."[1]

Mackey goes on to say:

> No relation can be traced between the Operative Masons of this class and the Speculative Mason, who represented Freemasonry since the beginning of the 18th century.[2]
>
> The first Masons were builders, they could have been nothing else. To seek for them in a mystical, religious association as the ancient Pagan Mysteries, or in an institution of chivalry as the Knights of the Crusades would be a vain and unprofitable task. As well might one look for the birthplace of the eagle in the egg of the crow as to attempt to trace the origin of Freemasonry to anything other than an association of builders.[3]
>
> It has been a favorite theory with several German, French, and British scholars to trace the origin of Freemasonry to the Mysteries of Paganism, while others, repudiating the idea that the modern association should have sprung from them, still find

analogies so remarkable between the two systems as to lead them to suppose that the Mysteries were an offshoot from the pure Freemasonry of the Patriarchs. In my opinion there is not the slightest foundation in historical evidence to support either theory.[4]

Melvin Johnson is somewhat more caustic in his ridicule of attempting to trace Masonry back to ancient times. For example,

It has been argued that Freemasonry began with the Mayans and Quiches in the Western Hemisphere much more than one hundred centuries ago; and that the mysteries migrated to the old world over a land bridge that was broken when Atlantis was destroyed. This theory is purely fanciful and pabulum only for the dreamer.[5]

Delmar Darrah explains why people believe such ridiculous tales:

It should not be overlooked that much of the literature and alleged history of Freemasonry consists mainly of abortive attempts to connect the fraternity through its symbolism with the mysteries of the ages, and in many instances a direct association has been made with crude ceremonies of an almost forgotten past. It is quite easy to understand the reason for this. The human mind loves the marvelous, and one of its greatest susceptibilities is to try and connect the vague and unknown with some supernatural agency and, as far as possible, link it with a mystical past thereby taking it out of the common place and enveloping it in a sort of etherial atmosphere.[6]

Freemasonry bears not the slightest resemblance to those ancient mysteries and mystical societies which in time past emanated from superstitious minds in turbulent periods of the world.[7]

The Masonic archaeologist who locates the origin of Masonry in the early periods of the world always fails to explain just how it was preserved through the hundreds of years precedent to its appearance in semi-organized form at the commencement of the eighteenth century, which proves conclusively that many of the written works on the antiquity of Masonry are simply based upon hasty assumption and untenable proposition. It was conjectures such as these cited which drew from Hallam, the most impartial of all historians, the derisive criticism that, "The curious subject of Freemasonry has unfortunately been treated only by panegyrists and calumniators each equally mendacious."[8]

Darrah goes on to point out that the pagan mystery elements in the higher Masonic degrees are of recent origin and have nothing to do with the issue of when and where Masonry started.[9]

Several other Masonic writers have attempted to set the record straight that Freemasonry did not come from ancient pagan religions or mysteries.

One such writer would be J. W. Mitchel. In 1871, in opposition to Pike, he refuted the idea that the Craft was a product of ancient mystery religions.[10]

Another such writer would be H. L. Haywood. In

his book *More About Masonry*, he states that "no evidence of any historical connection between the last Mystery and the earliest lodges has ever been discovered."[11]

Haywood points out that all the wild tales about the Craft coming from ancient mystery religions, Hindu gurus, Tibetan Masters, etc., have one thing in common:

> Though they differ among themselves to the very extremes of difference, though there have been hundreds of them, they one and all have in common the one point, *that they ask a Freemason to believe that Freemasonry was never itself but always something in disguise.* It is because they make this impossible demand on our credulity that none of these theories can be true. The whole story of the origin of our Fraternity can be told in a sentence of six words: *Freemasonry was founded by the Freemasons.* The Freemasons who erected the Abbey Church of St. Denis at Paris, or Cologne Cathedral, or York Minster were Freemasons and they themselves knew it; they knew that they were not Crusaders or Assassins, or Maya Indians in disguise. The Brethren knew that they had taken the Masonic obligation and not a Brahmin or a Druidic obligation. Nowhere in the records embodied in the Frabic Rolls, or the Borough Records, or old Minutes, or in the Proceedings of the First Grand Lodges are references anywhere made to alchemy, or Kabbalism, or astrology, or Rosicrucianism but they invariably are Masonic records. We ourselves who now belong to the Fraternity know who and what we are, and it would never cross our minds that we could be Druses, or Crusaders, or Jesuits without knowing it.[12]

Conclusion

Enough has been documented for the intelligent Mason to know that he has been misled by those occultic writers who for their own purposes have invented spurious pagan origins for the Craft. To be a Mason does not mean you have to leave Christianity and convert to Albert Pike's Hinduism or Manly P. Hall's occultism.

It is no wonder to us that those Masons who have been pressured to give up their faith in order to advance to the higher degrees feel robbed. The Lodge is supposed to be neutral and not a pagan temple of occult mysteries that some pretend it to be.

5

HISTORICAL ORIGINS

Trying to unravel the true historical origins of Freemasonry is a difficult task. We are reminded of an interesting legal case several years ago that involved the sale of a "Persian" carpet that was actually made in the USA.

During the trial, the following points were established:

1. The pattern on the carpet was indeed an ancient Persian design that had been used in that section of the world for centuries.

2. The wool used in making the carpet came from Turkey.

3. The dyes used in coloring the wool came from Egypt.

4. It was made by a Navaho on an Indian reservation.

5. This reservation was in the United States.

The controversy centered on whether the carpet could be labeled Persian, Turkish, Egyptian, Native American Indian, or just plain "Made in the USA." It all depended on how you looked at it. The seller argued that since the design of the carpet was a pattern used in ancient Persia, it could be sold as a "Persian" carpet. Its distinctive pattern should determine its name. As a matter of fact, carpets made in Iran, India, Turkey, and Afghanistan have been sold as "Persian" carpets for years. Persia as a nation does not exist anymore.

It was objected that this was fraudulent because it would give the buyer the idea that the carpet was several centuries old and came from ancient Persia when in reality it was made in 1965 in the USA. Things really got involved when it was then suggested that the same carpet could be sold as a Turkish, Egyptian, or Native American carpet.

The judge ruled that the carpet could only be sold as "Made in the USA" because it was made in the United States. It could not be sold as a Turkish or Egyptian carpet because many things made in this country used parts made in other nations. Neither could it be legitimately called "Native American" art because the design was Persian and not Navaho.

In the same way, when the average Mason asks, "Where did Freemasonry come from? When did it begin? And who started it?" he wants a straightforward answer. He does not want "mysteries" and "secrets." He wants the truth, plain and simple.

When he turns to modern Masonic writers, he is confronted with such a bewildering array of conflicting claims that he often shakes his head in utter confusion. Instead of scholarship, he is given fraudulent documents. Instead of honesty, he is fed lies. Instead of facts, he gets fantasies.

Let us for once cut through all the confusion and present the clear facts concerning the origins of modern Freemasonry.

Fact #1

What we call "Freemasonry" today should actually be called "Speculative Masonry" and it should be distinguished from "Operative Masonry."

Operative Masonry refers to those men who were actually engaged in the craft of stone masonry. They built stone houses, churches, bridges, government buildings, etc. As with any other trade during the Middle Ages, there was a guild of stone masons who traveled from one building site to another.

The few references to them in literature from that period reveal that they did not meet in Lodges. Furthermore, they did not have any of the degrees, symbols, rituals, or secrets which are found in modern Speculative Masonry.

It is also clear from the literary evidence that they considered themselves devout Christians and did not think of themselves as druids, witches, Mayans, pagans, worshippers of Isis or some other ancient deity. There was nothing cultic or occultic about them whatsoever.

Fact #2

According to all the hard evidence, the beginning of Speculative Masonry must be dated as June 24, 1717, when the Grand Lodge of London was organized at the Goose and Gridiron Tavern.

Those Masons who want to pretend that the Lodge began long before 1717 have referred to this first meeting as the "Revival of Freemasonry." But this is not historically accurate as Dr. Mackey points out.

Was the organization of the Grand Lodge in 1717 a Revival? It has been the practice of all Masonic writers from the earliest period of its literature to a very recent day, to designate the transaction which resulted in the organization of the Grand Lodge of England in the year 1717 as the "Revival of Freemasonry."

But this creed, popular as it is, has within a few years past been ruthlessly attacked by some of our more advanced thinkers, who are skeptical where to doubt is wise, and who are not prepared to accept legends as facts, nor to confound tradition with history.

And now it is argued that before the year 1717 there never was a Grand Lodge in England, and, of course, there could have been no Quarterly Communications. Therefore, as there had not been a previous life, there could have been no revival, but that the Grand Lodge established in June, 1717, was a new invention, and the introduction of a system or plan of Freemasonry never before heard or seen.[1]

After sifting through all the evidence, Mackey finally concludes that,

prior to the year 1717, there never were Grand Masters or a Grand Lodge except such as were mythically constructed by the romantic genius of Dr. Anderson.[2]

In the establishment of a Grand Lodge with quarterly meetings and an annual one in which a Grand Master and other Grand Officials were elected for the following year, we find no analogy to anything that had existed previous to the year 1717. We cannot, therefore, in these points call the organization which took place in that year a "Revival."[3]

Mackey points out that as early as 1870, Brother W. P. Buchan refuted the idea that the Lodge was "revived" in 1717. Buchan argued that all the degrees, symbols, gripes, rituals, offices, etc. connected with modern Freemasonry were unknown before the eighteenth century.[4] This was also argued in 1871 by Brother J. W. Mitchel in his work *The History of Masonry*.

After examining more than 200 books dealing with the history of Freemasonry, we failed to find a single author who was able to submit any hard evidence that the Lodge existed prior to 1717.

If the Lodge had existed "from the dawn of history," why did the early Masons have to meet in taverns instead of having their own meeting halls?

Dr. Mackey points out that the first Masonic hall in France was not built until 1765. London built its first hall in 1776. And the first Masonic hall in America was not erected until 1832. But even then some Lodges were still meeting in taverns well into the twentieth century.

It is also interesting to point out that these men built Masonic *halls*—not *temples*. The meeting places of Masons were not called "temples" until such writers as Albert Pike turned the Fraternity into "the religion of Freemasonry." Calling the meeting place a "temple" is a clear violation of the Landmarks.

If Freemasonry existed long before the establishment of the Grand Lodge in 1717, why has no one ever found any evidence of it? The truth of the matter is that if such evidence existed, there would have been no reason for Masonic writers to invent fraudulent documents. The presence of such frauds is clear proof of the absence of any clear evidence of antiquity.

We cannot leave this point without referring to the Baal's Bridge Square which is still used as proof by some writers that the Lodge existed before 1717. The Masonic inscription claims to have been written in 1507. But this must be viewed as a fraud because it uses "the" instead of "ye" when the English language of the 1500s used "ye." This fact was revealed by London Lodge No. 2076 in its 1969 *Transactions of Quator Coronati*. The Masonic inscription placed on Baal's Bridge is just another fraudulent attempt to manufacture antiquity for the Lodge.

Fact #3

When Freemasonry began in 1717, it was established as a "gentleman's club" which met from time to time in various taverns. This was nothing new or startling. Hundreds of such clubs were established during this period with many of them still in operation today.

Such clubs were places where rich and powerful gentlemen could meet to talk, drink, smoke, play cards, or just sit and read the paper. Of course, no women were ever allowed in such clubs.

We must remember that although the Christianity of the early Masons was orthodox, it was also quite shallow. It was, in many respects, more cultural than religious. This explains why they did not see any problem with calling themselves "Christians" and smoking cigars and drinking liquor at the same time.

The first Grand Lodge was established by and for the upper class. Thus it is no surprise that the first Masonic "club" or Lodge was led by the aristocracy such as the Duke of Montague, who became the Grand Master in 1721. A real stonemason with dirt under his fingernails would not have made it past the front door!

The clergymen and the aristocracy who made up the bulk of the membership in the early years of Freemasonry had never known a hard day's labor. They did not know anything about the art of stone masonry. They even had to hire non-Masons to build their halls as no builders were Masons!

Fact #4

The two most formative influences on early Masonry were the two Anglican clergymen, Dr. James Anderson and Dr. John Desagulliers. As Darrah points out, "It is to Anderson and John Theopilus Desagulliers, that we are indebted from the present system of Freemasonry."[5]

Dr. James Anderson was not a Deist as some have claimed. He even wrote a book defending the doctrine of the Trinity, a doctrine which no Deist would defend.

When Anderson joined the Lodge is not known. But he was asked in 1721 to draw up a Constitution for the Lodge. This he completed in 1723 under the title *Book of Constitutions*.

Although Anderson's book is still read by many Masons, Mackey warns that it,

> is fanciful, unreliable, and pretentious to a degree that often leads to absurdity. No Masonic writer would now venture to quote Anderson as authority for the history of the Order.[6]

While the Englishman Anderson has received most of the glory due to his book, it is thought by many that the true genius behind the setting up of Speculative Masonry was the Frenchman John Desagulliers who in 1719 became the third Grand Master. So esteemed was he that he was chosen to initiate the Prince of Wales into the Lodge. Desagulliers was also responsible for introducing Freemasonry in France and elsewhere in Europe.

Fact #5

One will search in vain to find any references to pagan mysteries or deities in early Freemasonry. We could not find a single reference to the occult arts such as magic or astrology. No one claimed to be a druid or a witch.

The first writer who tried to connect pagan mysteries with Freemasonry was the French writer Abbe Robin in 1780. He claimed that Masonry was the present guardian of the ancient mysteries.

Robin's theory was later picked up and defended by Alexander Lenoir, the French archeologist, in 1814. All the French Masonic writers followed Lenoir except for Rebold who argued that the Roman Colleges were the real origin of Freemasonry and not the ancient mystery religions.[7]

The French idea that Freemasonry was a continuation of ancient pagan mysteries did not really influence English Masonry until Godfrey Higgins in 1836 wrote his *Anacalypsis*. Higgins "borrowed" much from Lenoir's work.

Higgins believed that ever since the beginning of the world, there has always been only one true religion. But this religion has always been a "secret" told only to a few leaders of every race and religion. Because the average person cannot understand it, it was hidden and disguised under popular religions. All the great Masters from Buddha, Moses, Jesus, Zoroaster, Mohammed, the Tibetan Monks, etc. knew the secret teachings but did not reveal them to the masses.

Freemasonry is the "hidden church" which has carried the secret teachings of the ancient mysteries down through the centuries. Of course, as with all such groundless ideas, it was claimed that all the evidence for this theory was destroyed. In this way, the writer never has to prove anything.

Higgins' theory was repeated by A. T. C. Pierson and Godfrey W. Steinbrenner in 1865 in their book *The Traditions, Origin and Early History of Freemasonry*.

Finally in 1874, Albert Pike put together all the French Masonic writers from Robin to Eliphas Levi with such English writers as Higgins, Pierson, etc. and wrote his famous *Morals and Dogma*.

During the 1920s, the French myth that Freemasonry was actually an ancient secret pagan mystery religion was championed by dozens of writers such as Manly P. Hall.

Today, nine out of ten books on the nature and origin of Freemasonry will simply repeat the ideas of Albert Pike who plagiarized them from Higgins, Levi, Lenoir, Robin, etc.

As H. L. Haywood pointed out, all such "anacalyptic theories" are without the slightest foundation. They all contradict each other and not one of these writers has ever set forth a single proof of their claims. They all assume that Freemasons are really pagan priests in disguise. Haywood concludes,

> We now have a great mass of documents and other records, and the mass is growing rapidly; nowhere in the whole of it is there a hint that at any time in its long history the Fraternity has ever been anything more or anything other than the Fraternity of Freemasonry.[8]

Fact #6

The ceremonies, gripes, and teachings of present-day Freemasonry slowly came into the Craft from many different sources over a long period of time. The symbolism of the Craft did not drop out of heaven already complete but it slowly evolved to where it is today. As two well-known, modern Masonic scholars, Douglas

Knoop and G. P. Jones, put it, "Our present rites and ceremonies were built up gradually."[9]

In a "Letter Touching Masonic Symbolism," dated November 8, 1889, Albert Pike pointed out that there is no evidence that the early Masonry had any degrees or symbols until somewhere around 1726–1730. Even then, the Lodge had only one degree in the beginning.

In his massive work on Masonic symbolism, Pike stated,

> It is now certain that there were no degrees in Masonry 200 years ago; and that the Master's degree is no more than 150 years of age.[10]

Most Masonic historians now admit that it was Desagulliers or Anderson who invented the first three degrees. The Royal Arch was only a part of the third degree.

The few symbols introduced by these two Christian clergymen came from the Bible and were "Christian" in every sense. There is no evidence that they were pagans, Luciferians, or astrologers.

Most Masons will be surprised to discover that more than 3000 different Masonic degrees and more than 800 Masonic symbols have been introduced at one time or the other. It was quite popular at one time for lodges to have 90 degrees instead of only 33 degrees.

Most of the higher degrees and occultic symbols came from the French Lodges. As we have already pointed out, Albert Pike followed the French Lodge in its higher degrees in his revision of the Scottish Rite. Up until Albert Pike, the English Lodge had the greatest influence on American Masonry. But after Pike, one can clearly see the occultic stance of the French Lodge beginning to influence American Masonry.

Fact #7

Just as Freemasonry is a composite institution with rites and symbols derived from many different sources, the schism between the French and English Lodges reveals that it developed along different lines in different countries.

In England and in Scandinavia, Freemasonry has always been connected with the upper classes, with the aristocracy and with royalty itself. For example, the Kings of Sweden have generally been loyal Masons. From the very beginning, English Masonry has always had many notable clergymen in its ranks. The idea that they would permit the worship of Satan or Isis in the English Lodge is ridiculous.

German Freemasonry has always had a strong military membership. That the German Illuminati took it over for a while and used it for revolutionary ends is no surprise. Hitler made a point of dissolving it as he perceived it as a threat to the unity of the Third Reich.

Swedish Masonry, despite its connection to royalty, fell under the spell of the occultist Emanuel Swedenborg for a while, and some of his teachings can still be found in the higher degrees. But Swedenborgianism did not influence other national lodges as it did in Sweden.

While Masonry in France at first attracted the aristocracy, it soon became a hotbed of antiaristocracy, anticlerics, and antichurch radicals such as Voltaire. It became the home of skeptics, atheists, astrologers, magicians, Rosicrucians, and occultists of every stripe.

The evidence is clear that French Freemasonry did play a role during the French Revolution. Needless to say, the English aristocracy took somewhat of a dim view of what they called Jacobite Freemasonry.

The atheistic and skeptical leaders of the Lodge even went so far as to renounce the first Landmark of Freemasonry which is belief in God. They reinterpreted the "G" as a reference to Geometry instead of God. A. E. Waite comments,

> The bourgeois dynasty of Napoleon fell forever in 1870 and the infidel republic rose, widowed of the Divine Spouse and without God in the world. It transpired therefore in 1877 that as not one in the Grand Orient [Lodge] believed in God, that as religion was synonymous with priestcraft...the Name and Symbols of the Great Architect were removed from all the lodges.[11]

The Catholic Church responded to the attacks of French Masonry by declaring that no one could be a Catholic and a Mason at the same time. The Roman Church can hardly be faulted for defending itself from the vicious attacks of the Grand Orient Lodge.

When the French Masons threw God out of the Lodge, The Grand Lodge of London decreed that no member of the Grand Orient was welcome in their Lodges. In other words, no French Mason would be granted admittance into an English Lodge. The American Lodges followed suit and French Masonry was cut off from English Masonry.

The radical anticleric stance of French Masonry soon infected other Catholic countries such as Italy and Spain. This is why the Masonic Lodges in Italy were viewed with alarm by the Pope.

The French Lodge eventually dominated the Mexican, Central American, and South American Lodges. This is why they are known for being politically revolutionary and religiously anticleric and antichurch. It is no surprise that the great revolutionaries of Latin America such as Bolivar, O'Higgins, and Juarez were all Masons in the French Lodge. Freemasonry is so strong in some countries that every president has been a Mason.[12]

In America, although the Lodge was at first upper class, after the American Revolution, it became middle class and has remained so since that time. Good, solid, hardworking men compose the majority of the membership.

As in England, thousands of clergymen in America have been faithful members and officers in the Craft. The membership is basically Christian and not occultic or satanic. This is why until Albert Pike brought the symbols and degrees of the French Lodge into the Scottish Rite, American Masonry was not noted for being anticleric or antichurch.

Fact #8

Utter confusion reigns today over what is and is not a Masonic symbol and what a given symbol means. As W. H. Rylands stated,

> On very few questions has more rubbish been written than that of symbols and symbolism; it is a happy hunting ground for those who, guided by no sort of system or rule, ruled only by their own sweet will, love to allow their fancies and imaginations to run wild.[13]

For example, before World War II, the swastika was used as a Masonic symbol by those Masons influenced by the French Lodge. Such writers as Godfrey Higgins, Albert Pike, Manly P. Hall, and many other pagan masonic writers used the swastika as a Masonic symbol.[14] But what Mason today would accept the swastika as a valid Masonic symbol?

The two pillars and the dot in the circle have been interpreted in dozens of different ways. The most radical interpretation is from those Masonic writers who interpret such Masonic symbols as a reference to the male sex organ.[15]

This is a form of phallicism that is repulsive to the average person. Why such individuals must read the male sex organ into Masonic symbols is best left to the psychologists.[16]

Fact #9

There is a hidden agenda that motivates most of the modern books on Masonic symbolism. The writers will attempt to indoctrinate Masons into their pagan or occultic religion under the guise of it being the "secret, inner, deeper and true" meaning of the Masonic symbols.

If someone tells you that the historical interpretation of the two pillars is not true but that he is going to let you in on the "secret" meaning, he is lying—plain and simple. Some Masons appear to be little more than con artists only after your money or your soul. Freemasonry was never intended to brainwash people into occultic or cultic teachings.

Fact #10

The truth is that Freemasonry began as a gentlemen's club where all agreed not to debate such issues as religion or politics as this would generate strife. Today, Freemasonry is fast becoming a pagan occultic religion complete with its own temples, sacraments, and doctrines.

Far too many modern Masonic writers are anti-Christian bigots who try to brainwash their fellow Masons into accepting their occult teachings as the "true" meaning of Masonry.

It is time that good and honest Masons draw the line and say enough is enough. If they don't, Freemasonry will one day be a full-blown pagan religion where Christians are no longer welcomed or tolerated.

Conclusion

These 10 basic facts arise out of the evidence. To go beyond the evidence and to spin wild tales of ancient mysteries may be profitable in terms of book sales, but we would prefer the simple truth.

6

CONSPIRACY THEORIES

Down through the years, some writers have claimed that Freemasonry was part of a secret political or religious conspiracy. But since all of these writers disagree with each other as to the identity of this conspiracy, it makes us suspicious of any such claims.

Some of the conspiracy theories are just too outlandish to justify spending much time on them. When one writer tells you that Freemasonry is actually a Catholic plot to undermine Protestantism and another writer tells you that it is a Protestant plot to undermine Catholicism, something is seriously wrong. They cannot both be right.

After researching dozens of conspiracy theories, we have come to the following conclusions.

First, it is only natural that such a wealthy and influential organization as Freemasonry would be a target from time to time of individuals and groups who wished to use it for their own ends.

Second, that various groups have attempted to gain control of Freemasonry during its long history cannot be denied.

Third, while various groups have taken over individual Lodges or even a national Lodge, no group has ever been able to take control of every Lodge and every Mason in the world. For example, just because the Jacobites took over the Grand Orient Lodge and used it to promote the French Revolution, it would be erroneous to assume that they must have taken control of the English Lodge as well.

Fourth, Masonic conspiracies do not last long. They are overturned in time and the conspirators are vanquished to the pages of history.

Fifth, even after a conspiracy is long gone, elements from its brief presence in Masonry can remain in the Craft's symbolism and degrees. Some writers have mistakenly assumed that the presence of such elements proves that the conspiracy is still going on.

Sixth, we must avoid two extremes. On the one hand, we should not deny that Freemasonry has been influenced by various political and religious groups down through the years. The facts of history would be against any such denials. On the other hand, we should not claim that just because some group influenced parts of Freemasonry for a while in this or that country that this means that all Masons were and are still involved in this conspiracy to this very day. This is the basic error of most conspiracy theories.

Seventh, many Masons feel that it is high time to "clean house" in order to remove some of the more offensive elements left over in the symbolism and degrees of the Craft. We heartily concur with their feelings.

With these brief opening remarks, let us examine some of the conspiracy theories that still float around in Masonic circles.

The Illuminati Conspiracy

We have been told on several occasions by well-meaning individuals that Freemasonry is actually run by a secret political conspiracy called the Illuminati. This led us to investigate the history of the Illuminati Society.

The facts concerning this political conspiracy are not hard to uncover. It was a secret society started by Adam Weishaupt in 1776 in Bavaria. Its aims included the destruction of all national governments, patriotism, all established religions, private property, and the family unit in order to bring about a one-world government and one-world religion where peace and goodwill would reign over all people.

Of course, the aims of the society meant the destruction of the Christian church. As a former Catholic now into the occult, Weishaupt had a particular hatred of Catholicism. His plan to destroy the Church of Rome brought many radical Protestants into the group who failed to understand that the Protestant church was next on Weishaupt's hit list.

It had a particular appeal to military leaders in Bavaria, Germany, Holland, France, and Italy. More than 2000 rich and powerful members were initiated into the society. Most of them were not told the real goals of the society but they were fed the "one-world peace" idea as a trick to get their money.

From the very beginning, Weishaupt saw Freemasonry as the means whereby he could reach his political goals. Through his followers, Weishaupt took over hundreds of Lodges in several different countries. Mackey comments,

> To give [the society] influence it was connected with Freemasonry, whose symbolic degrees formed the substratum of its esoteric instructions.[1]

Its seditious character was uncovered when a Grand Master was struck dead by lightning while acting as a messenger for the Society. When his body was searched, secret papers telling of the Illuminati's plan to overthrow all governments and religions was discovered. This resulted in mass arrests and the eventual destruction of the Society.

The French and German Lodges were already deeply involved in the occult and were filled with anticlerics who saw in the Illuminati a way to crush Christianity.

The teachings of the Illuminati even reached all the way across the Atlantic and gained a small following in America. In 1798, Reverend Snyder sent a copy of Robison's book *Proofs of a Conspiracy*, which "gives a full Account of a Society of Free-masons, that distinguishes itself by the Name of Illuminati, whose Plan is to overturn all Government and all Religion" to President George Washington.

His first response which is dated September 25, 1798, dismissed the idea that the Illuminati had any influence on American Freemasonry. It is apparent from his letter that Washington had not read the book when he sent this response.

> Sir: Many apologies are due to you, for my not acknowledging the receipt of your obliging favour of the 22nd. I have heard much of the nefarious, and dangerous plan, and doctrines of the Illuminati, but never saw the Book until you were pleased to send it to me. I believe notwithstanding, that none of the Lodges in *this* country ascribed to the Society of the Illuminati.[2]

Washington's second response is dated October 24, 1798. It would seem that Washington finally got around to reading the book after Snyder wrote him again. What he read obviously alarmed him.

Revd Sir: I have your favor of the 17th instant before me; and my only motive to trouble you with the receipt of this letter, is to explain, and correct a mistake which I perceive the hurry in which I am obliged, often, to write letters, have led you into.

It was not my intention to doubt, the Doctrines of the Illuminati, and principles of the Illuminati, and principles of Jacobism had spread in the United States. On the contrary, no one is more truly satisfied of this fact than I am.

The idea that I meant to convey, was, that I did not believe that the Lodges of Free Masons in *this* Country had, as Societies, endeavored to propagate the diabolical tenets of the first, or pernicious principles of the latter (if they be susceptible of separation). That Individuals of them may have done it, or that the founder, or instrument employed to found, the Democratic Societies in the United States, may have had these objects; and actually had a separation of the People from their Government in view, is too evident to be questioned.[3]

Washington, like most American Masons, viewed the Illuminati as "diabolical" and "nefarious." Although the Illuminati had a few followers in America, their influence was small because, as in England, the members of the American Lodge were not occultists or anti-Christian bigots.

As would be expected, Albert Pike's view of the Illuminati was quite different from Washington's view. Pike had a positive opinion of the Illuminati. He even claimed that they had recovered the "lost" Masonic word![4]

The claim that Freemasonry is ruled today by the mysterious and secretive Illuminati Society is erroneous because the Illuminati no longer exists except in the minds of conspiracy theorists.

The Rosicrucian Conspiracy

One theory that has had many followers is the idea that Freemasonry was created by a secret occult society called the Rosicrucians or the Society of the Rosy Cross. It is also known as Hermetic Philosophy.

Mackey comments,

> Many writers have sought to discover a close connection between the Rosicrucians and the Freemasons, and some, indeed, have advanced the theory that the latter are only the successors of the former. Whether this opinion be correct or not, there are sufficient coincidences of character between the two to render the history of Rosicrucianism highly interesting to the Masonic student.[5]

One Masonic writer, F. Castells, complained in 1932 that too many Masons "fail to see the obvious connection between Freemasonry and the Rosy Cross."[6] He went on to claim that "Freemasonry was but an alias for Rosicrucianism."[7]

> Our thesis [is] that Freemasonry came through the [Rosicrucian] movement initiated by the Kabbalists.[8]

Castells claimed that such writers as Wigston, Bonneville, Bulhe, De Quincey, Parker, Soane, Woodford, Higgins, Pike, Sloane, Vaughan, and Pott all agreed that Freemasonry came from the Rosicrucians.[9] To this list we add Nicolai who was the most scholarly writer in this vein.

It is obvious that Masons who want to know the history of the Craft must examine the history and teachings of Rosicrucianism. But this is not as easy as it seems. The name "Rosicrucian" has been used by so many conflicting groups down through the years that one despairs of ever unraveling the true history of the name or the various movements which have used the title.

Secular historians generally agree that it was a movement started in the seventeenth century.[10] It was during this period that the Jewish Kabbalah was for the first time widely available. Its mixture of Jewish mysticism, sorcery, astrology, alchemy, and magic appealed to occultists throughout Europe.

The founder or founders were deeply involved in the occult arts. They put together an esoteric or secret teaching that combined elements from Jewish Kabbalism with Greek Gnosticism and Egyptian Hermetic religions. They formed secret societies where the adepts would be granted knowledge as they progressed through various degrees and rituals.

A comparison between Rosicrucianism and modern Freemasonry is quite revealing. In most Rosicrucian groups you will find Lodges, temples, secret hand gripes and signs, membership dues, progress through degrees, and secret teachings. A throne is set in the East end of the Lodge where the Grand Master sits, the East symbolizes light while the West symbolizes darkness, the candidate or adept enters by the West and faces the East, and he is initiated into the Lodge. They worship at an altar, wear strange vestments, use a rosy cross, jewels, triangles, circles, crystals, crosses, a Bible square and compass, etc.

It is rather obvious that, logically speaking, either the Rosicrucians borrowed from Freemasonry, the Freemasons borrowed from Rosicrucianism or they both borrowed from a third source. Not surprisingly, all three positions have had supporters.

Based on the historical evidence, we came to the following conclusions.

First, Rosicrucianism existed before Freemasonry began in 1717. It thus could not have borrowed anything from Freemasonry.

Second, Rosicrucian societies were in London as well as in Europe when Freemasonry began. They were separate and distinct from early Masonic meetings.

Third, as Mackey pointed out, early Masonry did not contain any Rosicrucian symbols, degrees, or teachings. They did not have any higher degrees. There is no evidence that they knew anything about Hermetic philosophy, the Kabbalah, or Gnosticism. In short, early Masonry did not come out of Rosicrucianism.[11]

Fourth, Mackey goes on to state that it was French Speculative Freemasonry which later on used Rosicrucianism as a guide in developing its higher degrees and symbolism.[12]

In "A Letter Touching Masonic Symbolism," Albert Pike agreed with Mackey that the early Masons were not Rosicrucians (p. 1). Hermetic philosophy did not enter Freemasonry until much later via French Masonry (p. 7).

> Philosophical-Symbolic Masonry means something quite different, in which the symbols conceal, and to the adept express, the great philosophic and religious truths of antiquity; or, it may be, the philosophic doctrines of the Hermeticists and Rosicrucians, these two being as their books show, the same (p. 1).

Pike and Mackey are not alone in seeing a Rosicrucian influence in the higher degrees. Bernard Jones stated, "It is just and proper to admit the possibility of our Craft degrees having been influenced by individual Rosicrucians."[13]

The French Lodge was already occultic and anti-Christian when it had an influx of Rosicrucians into Freemasonry. As Manly P. Hall stated, "It has been a mistake to disregard this influx of Rosicrucian apologists and operative Hermetic philosophers."[14]

After Mackey pointed out that such Masonic degrees as "the Knight of the Sun" came from the Rosicrucians, he goes on to state,

> But the Hermetic degree which to the present day has exercised the greatest influence upon the higher degrees of Masonry is that of the Rose Croix. This name was given to it by the French and it must be noticed that in the French language no distinction has ever been made between the Rosenkreutzer and Rose Croix.[15]

Gould in his *History of Freemasonry* (III:46ff.), traces the Rosicrucian elements in Freemasonry to French Masonry.

As we have already demonstrated, it was Albert Pike who used French Masonry which was built on Rosicrucianism which came out of the occult teachings of the Kabbalah to create the higher degrees in the Scottish Rite.

As A. E. Waite pointed out,

> The influence of the Rosicrucian Fraternity upon that of the Masons has been questioned only by those who have been unfitted to appreciate the symbolism which they

possess in common. It has been exercised more specially in connection with High Grades, as to which it is impossible—for example—to question that those who instituted the Eighteenth Degree of the Scottish Rite either must have received something by transmission from the old German Brotherhood or, alternatively, must have borrowed from its literature.[16]

It is interesting to note that The Rosicrucian Society with headquarters in the Rosicrucian Park, San Jose, California, denies that there is any connection between itself and Freemasonry.[17]

While this is true in an organizational sense, it cannot be denied that modern Freemasonry owed much of its degrees, symbolism, rituals, terminology, emblems, and even the floor plan of the Lodge to the Rosicrucians. But this was not a part of American Masonry until Albert Pike.

The American Revolution Conspiracy

Some writers have jumped to the conclusion that because Franklin, Washington, Paul Revere, and many other notable leaders of the American Revolution were Masons, the Revolution was therefore a Masonic conspiracy which came from the radical teaching of the Jacobites in the French Lodge.

While it is true that Franklin was made Grand Master in the French Lodge while in Paris, there is no evidence that Franklin's religious or political views changed after being in France. His deism and revolutionary views were no doubt applauded by French Masons. But he had these views before he went to France. His involvement in the French Lodge may have just been a wise political move to gain French support for the American Revolution.

Since American Masonry like the English Lodge appealed to the higher classes, it is no surprise to find that politicians, military leaders, wealthy businessmen, and influential clergymen were members of the Lodge. Since any political issue would naturally involve these kinds of men, it is no surprise to find Masons on both sides actively involved.

During the American Revolution, many "higher class" Masons were loyal to the Crown and had to flee to England, Canada, or the Bahamas. Other Masons such as Benedict Arnold actively worked against the Revolution.

Those Masons who were patriots like Paul Revere supported the Revolution. The bottom issue is whether these men were patriots because they were Masons or because they were Americans. To assume that they were for the Revolution only because they were influenced by French Masonry is not tenable once one considers the following facts.

First, there were not that many Masons in America. At the most, the Lodge had only 2000 members. The attempt to limit the Revolution to Masons is absurd. The support for the Revolution far exceeded the number of patriotic Masons.

Second, the American Lodge refused to admit French Masons before and after the Revolution. This would not have been the case if they were involved in a conspiracy with the Grand Orient Lodge.

Third, Franklin was virtually the only American Mason to have direct contact with the French Lodge. We failed to find any link between the French Lodge and other leaders of the Revolution.

Fourth, French Masonry was anticleric, anti-Christian and occultic as well as antiaristocracy. If French Masonry was the ideological source of the ideals of American Revolution, why is there no evidence of these things in the American Revolution? The clergy were at the forefront of the war even in Washington's army. If the churches had not been behind the Revolution, it would have failed.

Fifth, since the Scottish Presbyterians and the Baptists were in the forefront of the Revolution, their statements about why they were patriots must be taken seriously. It is clear that they did not look to the ghastly horrors of the French Revolution as their inspiration. Instead, they looked to the Scottish Presbyterian Revolutions against the religious tyranny of England for their inspiration.

Simply stated, there is no solid evidence that the American Revolution was a conspiracy rigged by American Masons under the influence of the radicals in the French Lodge. As with all such conspiratorial theories, it is based on a vivid imagination, a tremendous amount of guesswork and a pile of half-truths.

Masonic writers such as Fäy, Roth, Tatsch, and Morse have done great damage to the credibility of Masons by perpetuating certain myths about the degree of Masonic involvement in the American Revolution. They have given much fuel to those who love conspiracies. To combat the spread of the half-truths and out-and-out lies, Delmar Darrah, John C. Smith, Melvin Johnson, and other Masonic writers have been willing to expose these myths for what they really are.[18]

Some of these myths are as follows:

1. It is a myth that all the signers of the Declaration of Independence were Masons. Out of the 55 signers, only five or six were Masons according to any hard evidence.

2. It is a myth that the Boston Tea Party was a Masonic act of a Boston Lodge. Out of the men involved, maybe two or three were Masons.

3. It is a myth that all of Washington's generals were Masons.

4. It is a myth that George Washington forced General LaFayette to become a Mason in order to fight in the Revolution. LaFayette claimed that he had become a Mason in France when a young man.

5. It is a myth that Washington was a loyal Mason who faithfully attended his Lodge. The plain fact is that Washington was elected to Masonic offices, given various Masonic honors, and even had his portrait painted in full regalia without his knowledge, approval, or even presence! When informed of such actions, he would withdraw himself from the honors conferred.

After being informed that he had been elected Grand Master over all the Lodges in America, Washington refused to accept the office. In a letter dated September 25, 1798, Washington stated,

> And which allows me to add little more now, than thanks for your kind wishes and favourable sentiments, except to correct an error you have run into, of my Presidency over the English lodges in this Country. The fact is, I preside over none, nor have I been in one more than once or twice, within the last thirty years.[19]

The truth is that Washington became a Mason in his youth but never attended much. His prominence in the Revolution and the presidency gave Masons the chance to boast about his being a Mason. But this does not erase the fact that he had not attended a Lodge meeting more than once or twice in 30 years! He rejected his election to the office of Supreme Grand Master of all Lodges. In short, he was not a faithful Mason.

Also, there is no hard evidence to support all the stories of Washington marching around the Capital City in full Masonic regalia laying the cornerstones of virtually every government building from the Congress to the White House. These myths make good stories but are actually quite worthless.

Swedenborgian Conspiracy

All the European scholars such as Findel, Lenning, Reghellini, Ragon, and Thory clearly saw the influence of Swedenborg in the higher degrees. In America, the Masonic historian Beswick wrote extensively on this theme as early as 1870. This has led some people to think that Freemasonry is part of a Swedenborgian conspiracy.

Emanuel Swedenborg (1688–1772) was perhaps the greatest occultist of his time. Without a doubt, he was a genius and wrote extensively on hundreds of subjects from science to religion. He was subject to fits and seizures during which he heard voices and saw visions. He interpreted these experiences as God calling him to establish a new church built on new doctrines revealed through him. In his dreams/visions he claimed to have visited heaven and hell and even witnessed the Apocalypse, i.e., the Second Coming of Christ and the end of the world.

His followers later developed Masonic symbols and degrees which taught Swedenborg's ideas. From the evidence, it is clear that the occultic teachings of Emanuel Swedenborg had an influence on Freemasonry in Scandinavia. The question before us is whether Swedenborg borrowed his ideas from Freemasonry or was it the other way around?

Mackey argued that Swedenborg did not borrow his occultic system from Freemasonry.

> If there was really a borrowing of one from the other, and not an accidental coincidence, it was the Freemasons of the high degrees who borrowed from Swedenborg, and not Swedenborg from them. And if so, we cannot deny that he has unwittingly exercised a powerful influence on Masonry.[20]

The Apocalyptic 17th Degree in the Scottish Rite came from Swedenborg via Albert Pike. In his work *Morals and Dogma*, Pike tells us,

> Masonry is a search for Light. That search leads us directly back, as you see, to the Kabalah. In that ancient and little understood medley of absurdity and philosophy, the Initiate will find the source of many doctrines; and may in time come to understand the Hermetic philosophers, the Alchemists, all the Anti-papal Thinkers of the Middle Ages, and Emanuel Swedenborg (p. 741).

Pike used the ideas, symbols, and degrees that he found in Kabbalism, Hermeticism (which is another name for Rosicrucianism), magic, sorcery, anti-Christian bigotry, and Emanuel Swedenborg.

While it is clear that the influences of Swedenborg can still be found in the symbolism and teachings of the higher degrees, we should not attempt to weave together some kind of conspiracy theory out of these elements.

Occult Conspiracies

If we had the time, we could go on to examine how the occult arts such as magic, astrology, and alchemy found their way into the symbols and rituals of the higher degrees. One interesting question which every Lodge should discuss is why should modern Masons be involved in such superstitions?

Another good question to ask is how and by whom has the occultic doctrine of pantheism worked its way into the teachings of Freemasonry when it clearly contradicts the first Masonic Landmark?

From the very beginning Freemasonry was committed to belief in a *personal* God whom they called "the Great Architect." He was viewed as the Creator of all things and thus was Himself not a "thing." He is a personal God who hears and answers prayer. This is why prayer has always been a vital part of Masonry.

On the other hand, pantheism is the denial that such a personal God exists. It is thus a form of atheism which says that only the world exists. It then claims that the world is "god." Instead of believing in the Great Architect, a pantheist can only believe in Great Architecture!

Philosophically speaking, a "god" who is impersonal is an "it" deity who does not know that "it" exists or that we exist. It is of no use to pray to an "it" deity who cannot hear or respond. Thus all Masonic prayers are a worthless sham once the existence of the Great Architect is denied and a pantheistic doctrine takes its place.

How can a pantheist be a Mason when he denies the existence of the Great Architect? This question can no longer be avoided.

Conclusion

Any honest student of Masonry will admit that Freemasonry has suffered many attempts to take it over for diabolical ends. Alchemists, magicians, astrologers, mediums, reincarnationists, pagans, revolutionaries, anti-Christian bigots, pantheists, and others have taken an organization that was once compatible with Christianity, indeed influenced by Christianity, and turned it into something so occultic that the early Masons would not have joined it.

Is it possible to restore Freemasonry to its original purity? Yes, it is possible. Albert Pike radically altered the symbolism and teachings found in the higher degrees. And if one man could do this, cannot a group of men do it again? As Masonry enters the twenty-first century, maybe it is time for Masons to "clean house."

7

ANTI-MASONRY MOVEMENTS

Sooner or later, every Mason comes into contact with anti-Masonry books and pamphlets. It cannot be avoided.

While we will not attempt to equal Cerza's nearly 400-page discussion of anti-Masonry movements, we can give a brief overview of the history and nature of the accusations raised against the Craft.

Let us begin by understanding what kinds of motives make people into anti-Masons.

First, there are those who have *personal* reasons as to why they are against Freemasonry. Maybe they were in a Lodge where there was racial prejudice or where they did not get their way. Regardless of the reason, they have a personal ax to grind when it comes to the Lodge.

Second, there are those that have *political* reasons for attacking the Lodge. This is a particularly strong reason in Europe and Latin America where Masons are involved in politics. As Darrah pointed out,

> It cannot be denied that in various periods of the world the fraternity has been used by

designing men for political purposes and prior to the war of 1914, in several European countries where the fraternity maintained a precarious existence, it was under constant observation of state authorities lest its membership should become involved in intrigue and conspiracy against the government.

In France, Masonry has assumed political character due largely to the intense hatred of the French people against the Jesuits. This is equally true in all strong Roman Catholic countries.[1]

The recent political scandals in Italy which involved Masons is an example of what can motivate some anti-Masonry feelings.

Third, there are those who have sincere *religious* objections to the oaths, symbolism, degrees, and teachings of modern Freemasonry. This is the heart of most of the anti-Masonic movements in the United States.

There are three ways that anti-Masons attack the Lodge.

First, some anti-Masons have taken it upon themselves to publish all the secrets of the Lodge. According to Mackey, this was first done in 1730 by Samuel Prichard in his book *Masonry Dissected, Being an Universal and Genuine Description of All Its Branches from the Original to the Present Time*.[2] Since that time there have been dozens of books written by former Masons some of whom were thirty-third degree Masons that reveal everything. And when we say everything, we mean *everything*.

In all fairness, we must admit that there are no secrets left in the ritual of the Craft which have not been revealed to the general public by books, pamphlets, and now even by videotapes!

Delmar Darrah is bold enough to say,

> In the present age there is but little about the Masonic fraternity that is secret.
> The history of the fraternity is available to the public. Volumes have been written upon its symbolism; monitors have been published, in which much of the ritualistic work has been promulgated... there is very little concerning the fraternity which is not known to the public.[3]

Second, some anti-Masons attack Freemasonry for being a secret society which is viewed as dangerous, revolutionary and unpatriotic. They are usually opposed to all secret societies in principle.

In all fairness, we must state that Freemasonry is and is not a secret society at the same time. If by secret society one is referring to a group which attempts to keep its existence a secret, this is clearly not true of Masonry whose temples dot the land and whose members advertise their membership by rings and bumper stickers.

On the other hand, if one means an organization that tries to keep its inner workings, rituals, hand gripes, signs, and symbols a secret, then Freemasonry is guilty as charged. But to say that an organization does not have the right to keep anything secret is absurd. Every business and organization has its secrets.

Third, some anti-Masons focus on certain objectionable elements found in the rituals, symbols, and teachings of modern Freemasonry. This is the main way that modern anti-Masonry movements attack the Lodge.

The question which each honest Mason must ask himself is, What if the anti-Masons are right? What if they have found things in the present symbols, degrees, and teachings of Freemasonry which are truly offensive? Should Masons go on pretending that all is well or do they change whatever needs to be changed so as not to unnecessarily offend people?

Since most modern anti-Masonry movements are religiously motivated, we will limit our discussion to the religious objections to Freemasonry. Please note that we are not attacking any church or denomination. If a church is against the Lodge, Masons should listen long and hard to the objections raised. To be closed minded is not part of Masonic ethics.

The Catholics

The bitterest foe of Freemasonry has always been the Roman Catholic Church. The first time it spoke out against Masonry was in France in 1738. But there was just cause for this action as Darrah explains,

> In France and Italy, there has probably been just cause for the Roman Catholic Church to take up the cudgel against the Freemasons of those countries because of their political activities...this has been true in certain European countries where the Freemasons have used the fraternity as a political agency to wage war against the ever increasing power of the Church of Rome.[4]

After a long series of papal bulls against Freemasonry, the Catholics held an Anti-Masonic Congress at Trent in 1896 where, according to A. E. Waite, the following charges were made:

1. Freemasonry is anti-Christian.

2. Freemasonry is anti-religious.

3. Freemasonry is revolutionary in politics.

4. Freemasonry is a conspiracy to establish the religion of naturalism on the ruins of the Church.[5]

As we have already brought out in our study of Leo Taxil and his Luciferian Masonic conspiracy, the occultic anticleric revolutionaries who ran the French and Italian Lodges attacked the Catholic Church with great bitterness. It is not surprising that they were answered in kind.

According to *The New Catholic Encyclopedia*, the ban forbidding Catholics to join the Lodge still stands. The reason that thousands of Catholics can get away with being members of the Fraternity in the United States is that American priests look the other way just as they do with the Church's ban on birth control. Many devout Catholics still have qualms about joining an organization which is officially under papal condemnation.[6]

The Lutherans

The conservative Missouri Synod Lutheran Church issued its ban on Masonic membership in 1964.[7]

The reasons why they condemned Freemasonry are:

1. It is a religion as many Masonic writers declare.

2. It claims to have come from ancient pagan mystery religions which deny Christian doctrines.

3. It is universalistic and anti-Christian.

4. It teaches that salvation comes through works.

5. It downgrades the name of Christ.

6. It has a false view of God.

7. It denies the supremacy of the Bible by using other books.

8. It is a cult.

9. It forbids people to pray in the name of Jesus.

10. It is anti-Christian in its bloody oaths and secrets.

What Masons must understand is that these serious objections do not come out of thin air or from religious prejudice. We discovered that the committee which issued this report documented each charge by dozens of Masonic books.

In all fairness, we must admit that various Masonic writers such as Albert Pike have made anti-Christian statements which are offensive not just to Lutherans but to all Christians.

What we must ask ourselves as we enter the twenty-first century is, why cannot the Supreme Councils of all the various Masonic Rites officially condemn all anti-Christian bigotry? Why not remove those elements in the Craft which are offensive to Christians?

The Reformed

The Orthodox Presbyterian Church in 1942 and the Christian Reformed Church in 1974 condemned Freemasonry for basically the same reasons as the Lutherans did. Other Presbyterian bodies have followed the example of the Orthodox Presbyterians.[8]

Once again we find that these reports document each charge from Masonic writers. How can we find fault with their conclusions if they are quoting from books which are recommended by state Lodges?

The Fundamentalists

Next to the Catholics, those Christians who view themselves as evangelical or fundamentalists have had the longest history of being anti-Masonic.[9] The first time conservative evangelical and fundamental churches became openly anti-Masonic was in 1826 in connection with the murder of William Morgan.

Now that the dust has settled, the facts are clear that when a Mason by the name of William Morgan declared his intention to publish a book in which he would reveal all the secrets of the Lodge, a small group of Masons kidnapped him and then murdered him in order to keep the secrets safe. Of course, the book was later published. Morgan's murder only served to make it a bestseller!

Who today would hold all present Masons responsible for this heinous act? Neither should we hold all the Masons of 1826 guilty of murder. But the actions of a few misguided men brought all of Masonry to its knees in just a few years.

We spent a great deal of time examining all the court documents and books which came out of this regrettable incident. The records reveal that the governor of the state, the judges, and many of the law enforcement officers were Masons who felt they were duty-bound to protect these men even though they had murdered a man. The Masons who murdered Morgan received light sentences. They were able to move their own furnishings into their cells. The cell doors were not usually locked. They often went home for the weekends. One of them was even allowed to run a business from his cell. Regardless of how you look at it, such things do not seem consistent with the serious crime of murder.

Common Objections

Perhaps it would be wise at this point for us to summarize the common objections urged against Freemasonry by Christians. What should strike the average Mason is that all branches of the Christian Church from Catholics to fundamentalists are united in their objections to certain elements in the rituals and symbols of the Craft. Obviously there must be things in the ritual which are offensive to Christians. What are they?

The Bloody Oaths

The charges brought against Freemasonry usually begin with the bloody oaths. Most Masons today do not take these oaths seriously. If they did, it would make Masons as dangerous as Jim Jones or Charles Manson.

Since the oaths to commit murder by slitting someone's throat and then disemboweling him were not a part of early Freemasonry and are only remnants of the political conspiracies of the Illuminati and the Jacobites, why shouldn't they be revised or removed? After all, since their purpose was to scare people into keeping the secrets of the ritual secret, obviously the oaths did not work because there are no secrets left in Freemasonry!

Good and honest Masons must ask therefore why should the bloody oaths remain a part of the ritual when its very nature is objectionable not only on religious grounds but to any civilized man? Why not remove the offense?

Indeed, some Lodges are making changes in this very area. See "Recent Masonic Change" (pp. 118-120) for Pennsylvania's new ordinances regarding bloody oaths.

The God of Masonry

The early Masons tried to set up a gentleman's club which would be open to wealthy, upper-class Catholics and Protestants. Both of these religions based their ideas of God on the Bible and they believed in a personal God who, as the Creator of all things, was the Grand Architect to whom prayer could be addressed. These early prayers were distinctively Christian and ended with the phrase "in Jesus' name."

The God of Masonry at the beginning was the Christian Trinity of Father, Son, and Holy Spirit. The triangle was used as a symbol for the Trinity.

Since it is obvious that Jews as well as Christians believed in the personal Creator of the universe, they were later admitted to the club. At first, the Jewish members were told that while they did not have to participate in the Christian elements of the ritual, the Lodge was not going to change its ritual for them. We have already touched upon the case of Jacob Norton and the refusal of the Grand Lodge of Massachusetts to delete the Christian elements from its rituals just to please him.

As time went along, the name of Jesus Christ was gradually omitted from the prayers and rituals in many Lodges to accommodate the Jewish religion. A simple prayer to the personal God of the Bible was thought to be sufficient.

But where there were no Jewish members and all the members of the Lodge were Christians, they continued praying in the name of Jesus well into the twentieth century. Indeed, in many of the adoptive Lodges such as the Eastern Star, they are still praying in the name of Jesus and singing Christian hymns.

As the British Empire spread itself over the world, the rich and powerful of all cultures wanted to be in the "club." Thus while the "God" of Masonry at the beginning was the personal Creator found in the Bible, room had to be made for rich Muslims and Hindus whose views of God did not come from the Bible. The rituals of

Masonry were changed to accommodate Muslims and Hindus.

It is a rule of logic that if something means everything, it means nothing. The attempt to stretch the word "God" to accommodate every religion is an exercise in futility. Why?

How in the world can Hinduism's three billion gods be called the Great Architect? How can a pantheist who rejects the idea of a personal God who hears prayer believe in and pray to the Great Architect? And what about the mystics in the Craft who pray to Ra or Isis? Obviously, something has to give.

What has happened is that leading spokesmen of the Fraternity such as Albert Pike and many others like him became determined to de-Christianize the Craft by making it openly pagan and anti-Christian.

The proof of this is that while all other religions can pray in the name of their deity such as Allah, Buddha, Shiva, or Krishna, Christians are the only ones who are forbidden to pray in the name of their deity, Jesus Christ! If the Muslims can use the name of Allah, why can't the Christians use the name of Jesus? Has the Craft become anti-Christian?

As we demonstrated in the book *Battle of the Gods* (Southbridge, MA: Crowne Publishers, 1989), universalism has always been anti-Christian. When someone tells you that all religions are true and then turns around and says that Christianity is false, this is self-contradictory. To be told that Christians cannot use the name of Jesus but all other religions are free to use the name of their deity is obviously anti-Christian.

As it stands right now, the predominant view of God as given in Masonic books is openly pagan. The God of Christianity is ridiculed and Jesus Christ is reduced to the level of Krishna or Zeus. If the Lodge was truly neutral and universal in its view of God, then Christian Masons could use the name of Jesus just as easily as

Muslim Masons now use the name of Allah. But every modern Mason knows that while the name of Jesus is forbidden, he is free to use the name of Allah, Krishna, or Ra or any other deity he chooses. Any name but Jesus will do. We are not being prejudiced when we point out this sad reality. This is a matter of fairness. Why should the Christian Masons be singled out for ridicule and prohibition when they were the very ones who began the Fraternity? Does this seem just or fair?

Salvation

As we previously documented, the early Masons pointed to the life and death of Jesus Christ as the way of salvation. Elements of this can still be found in the third degree. Biblical phrases such as "regeneration," "redemption," "heaven," etc. were part of the rituals.

As a matter of record, the early Masonic funerals were decidedly Christian and referred to the departed Mason as going to heaven or the Great Lodge above through the redemptive work of Jesus Christ. Reincarnation or other pagan ideas of the afterlife were never part of the original Masonic funeral service.

Once the Christian doctrine of redemption through Jesus Christ was omitted from the rituals of the Craft, the pagan writers rewrote these rituals to teach that a Mason goes to heaven by virtue of his membership in the Lodge and his good works! This is highly offensive to Christians who believe that salvation is by God's grace and not by works.

Even more offensive is that the pagan doctrines of the preexistence of the soul and reincarnation are now being openly taught in many Lodges as the "true" teachings of the Craft.

It has yet to dawn upon the average Mason that the teaching of reincarnation denies the existence of both the Great Architect and the Great Lodge in heaven!

Such pagan ideas as reincarnation make a mockery of the Masonic rituals by denying what they stand for. See our book *Reincarnation and Christianity* (Minneapolis: Bethany House Publishers, 1980) for further details.

While pagan Masons are allowed to talk openly about what they believe is the way of salvation, Christian Masons are told to keep quiet about what they believe! Is this fair?

We thus arrive at a situation that is not just. Hundreds of Masonic books which attack Christianity and openly teach paganism are published, supported, and recommended by high officials, state Lodges, and supreme councils. We are told that this is proper because the Lodge should be universal in appeal and each Mason can interpret the word "God" and the symbols of the Craft anyway he wants.

But when a Christian Mason attempts to give a Christian interpretation of the rituals and symbols of the Craft, he is forbidden to do this! That this is true can be seen if we ask when was the last time that a Christian interpretation of the Craft was published, supported, and recommended by high officials, state Lodges, and supreme councils.

We have seen hundreds of Hindu, Buddhist, Gnostic, druid, occultic, New Age, Hermetic, etc. interpretations of the Craft but not one Christian interpretation! If we have missed such a book, please let us know. If Masonry is truly universal and open to all religions, then why is it closed to Christianity?

Since the Lodge was willing to change its rituals so that it would not offend Jews, Muslims, and Hindus, then why cannot it change its rituals so it does not offend Christians? Why not remove elements in the Craft that are offensive to Christians?

If the leaders of modern Masonry are willing to accommodate all religions except Christianity, then we must agree with the anti-Masons that Masonry has become anti-Christian.

The Mystery Cults

The teaching that Freemasonry began in the ancient pagan mystery cults has even found its way into the Masonic Bible. It permeates hundreds of Masonic books. Most modern Masons believe it because it is endlessly repeated.

How then can we find fault with the anti-Masons for saying that Freemasonry is a pagan anti-Christian religion? Masonic writers cannot have their cake and eat it too!

If Freemasonry is indeed the religion of the ancient mysteries, then it is a pagan religion. If it was the religion of the Aryan race as found in the Vedas, then it is a pagan religion. It is absurd to say that Freemasonry is not a religion and then to turn right around and say it is the ancient religion of Isis.

For every Masonic writer who says that Freemasonry is not a religion, there are five Masonic writers who claim that it is a pagan religion. While they may disagree as to which pagan religion, they all agree that Christianity is wrong and its teachings must not be allowed in the Lodge.

While Masonic writers like Pike, Wilmshurst, Hall, Herner, Claudy, Perkins, and Steinmetz are allowed to teach their pagan religion in Lodge meetings, the Christians are not allowed to do so. While pagan Masons can openly evangelize the membership and seek to gain converts in Lodge meetings, the Christians are told to keep quiet about their religion. This does not seem fair to us.

If Freemasonry was truly neutral when it came to religion like the Boy Scouts, A.A., or the YMCA, then why has it allowed Albert Pike to teach his Aryan religion, Manly P. Hall to teach his mystery religion, Perkins to teach New Age religion, etc.?

If Christianity cannot be openly taught in the Lodge, than neither should any other religion. But the fact that pagan religions are being openly taught in Lodge meetings reveals that Pike's anti-Christian bigotry which he picked up from the French Lodge has won the day so far as modern Masonry is concerned.

Recent Masonic Changes

As a response to the growing number of anti-Masonic books and recent condemnations made by various Christian denominations, Freemasonry has instituted sweeping changes in the Blue Lodge and in the fourth to the thirty-second degrees. For example, in the state of Pennsylvania, the following changes have been made.

1. As part of its "Solomon II Project," a major public relations campaign has been started to convince the public that Freemasonry is not a "secret organization." Masonic Lodges will now be open at certain times to the public.

It is argued that the Lodge is not a "secret organization" because its buildings are clearly marked, its members put Masonic bumper stickers on their cars, and road signs are placed at community entrances indicating that the Masons have a Lodge in that city.

But all these things miss the point. No one accuses the Lodge of being "secret" in the sense of hiding its existence. The anti-Masonic objection focuses on the "secret" rituals and teachings of the Lodge. This has not changed.

2. The Solomon II Project also states that Freemasonry is not a religion. But this claim is difficult to accept because the Masonic Bible on page 32 establishes

"beyond question the character of the Fraternity as a religious institution."

A. E. Waite stated in his *A New Encyclopedia of Freemasonry,*

> True Masonry remains a Church of God and one at the roots with the Catholic and Christian church (p. 479).

3. When a man asks to be admitted to the Lodge, a committee will come to his home and ask his wife if she gives her permission for her husband to become a Mason. If she refuses to give her blessing, he will not be admitted. But if she gives her permission, she will be reminded of this in the future when her husband begins to spend a great deal of time at the Lodge.

The problem with this is that the wife is not told to what she is to agree or not agree. In fact, she will never be told what transpires in the Lodge when it is closed to the public.

4. Since the major objection of many churches to Freemasonry focuses on the bloody oaths, it has been decided to modify them. Instead of the bloody oaths, the new ritual uses the words "censured, suspended or expelled" as the penalty for revealing the secrets of the Lodge. This change is clearly in the right direction.

During the Lecture in the East, the following words are now used:

> This is the sign of the...degree. It is of ancient origin and symbolic only and will be explained to you at a later time.

Those anti-Masonic books which used the bloody oaths as the basis of their objection to Freemasonry must now be updated or face being irrelevant.

5. Since so many men had a problem memorizing the rituals so they could move up from the fourth to the

thirty-second degree, it was decided in the late 1960s that it was no longer necessary for Masons to participate personally in the rituals. Instead, the rituals are performed on a stage in front of them. Thus they do not have to memorize anything.

6. It has now been decided that Masons do not have to move up to the higher degrees one degree at a time. The fourth to the thirty-second degrees would now be conferred in two weekends.

After six to eight hours of stage plays in which only some of the rituals are performed, all the degrees, including the thirty-second degree, are granted to the entire group that is present. It is thus no longer necessary to go through all the degrees in order to receive the thirty-second degree.

Conclusion

When Christian Masons complain that they are being singled out for ridicule by Masonic writers who then try to convert them to some pagan religion in the name of Freemasonry, it would seem to us that they have a legitimate cause to complain.

As we enter the twenty-first century, the Fraternity must decide just where it is going. Is it going to become Pike's Aryan religion complete with pagan temples, baptism, confirmation, and funeral services?

If Masonry continues to go in the direction it seems to be heading, then Christian Masons must leave the Craft because it has become an occultic pagan religion hostile to Christianity. It will no longer be a fraternity of good-hearted men. Instead, it will be just another cult with Eastern religious ideas. Is this the future of Freemasonry?

May we be so bold as to offer a suggestion? Why not call for a conference with anti-Masonic leaders to discuss what exactly offends them in Freemasonry and what can be done to remove those offenses. Why cannot Freemasonry change its rituals to accommodate the feelings of Christians just as it did for Jews, Muslims, and Hindus?

If the answer is that no changes will be made in Freemasonry in order to remove those elements offensive to Christians, then every Christian Mason must leave the Craft. He will no longer feel welcome.

8

CONCLUDING
THOUGHTS

W e have examined the major issues touching upon the origins, history, and teachings of Freemasonry. To do so, we have had to deal mostly with the past history of the Craft. But what of its future as it enters the twenty-first century?

Unless something radically happens to alter the present trends, Freemasonry will not enter the new century in a healthy state. To put it bluntly, Freemasonry is dying.

In *The Northern Light*, Arthur Sharp explains not only are there few new members being added but also the present membership is either dying off or quitting in alarming numbers. His study reveals that this is true for both the Northern and Southern Jurisdictions.

> Since 1957, symbolic Freemasonry in the Jurisdiction has been experiencing declining membership. This is happening because the fraternity is initiating fewer and fewer new members.[1]

Sharp gave the following two diagrams which illustrate the dramatic decline in membership in both Jurisdictions.

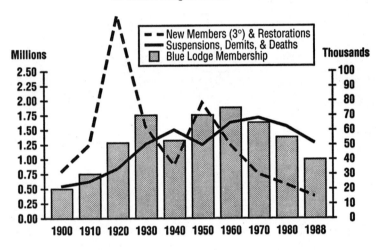

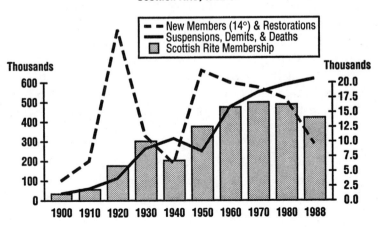

Sharp points out that,

> If the membership performance trends dur-
> ing the past 30 years prevail in the future,
> symbolic Freemasonry may expect to lose
> 45–50 percent of the existing membership
> before the year 2000.[2]

Membership statistics reveal that while the Fraternity grew 266 percent from 1900 to 1920, it has
declined almost 30 percent since 1959!

Sharp is not the only one concerned about the
decline in membership. W. Scott Stoner, the Grand Master of the Masons in Pennsylvania, pointed out that the
Masons were now going to run advertisements on TV
and radio in the hope of bringing in new members. He
has hired a Boston public relations firm to run radio, TV,
and newspaper campaign ads.

The article reporting this goes on to state,

> Stoner's decision to go public coincides with a
> dramatic decline in membership at all levels
> of the organization. Like many once prom-
> inent fraternal organizations—the Loyal
> Order of Moose, the Benevolent Protective
> Order of Elks, the Odd Fellows—the Masons
> are graying. Older members are dying faster
> than new ones are coming in.[3]

What worries Scott is the fact that in 28 years, one-
third of the Pennsylvania Masons have either died or
quit and no one has taken their place.

Robert S. Swoyer, District 10 Deputy Grand Master
comments, "It seems that younger people don't have as
much interest."[4]

Freemasonry is dying before our eyes. Because of
this fact, the Craft is now going to advertise openly in

order to get new members. Whether this will work has yet to be seen. But this act of "evangelism" which clearly violates the Landmarks reveals how truly desperate the situation has become.

The closest Lodge to us is practically dead. It is populated by five or six elderly gentlemen who cannot even afford to keep up the utilities on their building. They do not have regular meetings during the winter to save on heating. No new members have shown up in years.

The Root Problem

While there are no doubt many contributing reasons for this decline, may we be so bold as to suggest what we think to be the root problem? As the charts demonstrate, the underlying problem that is behind the present decline began in the 1920s when the leaders of Masonry started their crusade to de-Christianize the Craft and to put various pagan religions in its place.

To put it bluntly, there is a direct correlation between the increase of anti-Christian bigotry in the Craft and the decrease in membership. The more anti-Christian the Craft has become, the more it is out of line with the general population which is still Christian.

In other words, the Craft has been filled with a mumbo-jumbo world of ancient mysteries, Isis worship, fertility cults, phallicism, ancient pagan deities, sorcery, magic, astrology, reincarnation, crystals, Aryan Hinduism, and other pagan religions. Modern Freemasonry has "weirded out" on us.

While every nut-case and kook with weird religious views has found in Freemasonry a bloody pulpit to expound his religious fantasies, the Christians in the Craft are made to feel like second-class citizens who are told to keep quiet about what they believe and not to use the name of Jesus Christ in the Lodge! They are supposed to sit quietly by while Christianity is attacked, ridiculed, and vilified. No wonder they are leaving in droves!

A Possible Solution

There is no just reason under God's heaven why modern Freemasonry cannot remove those elements in its symbols and rituals which are blatantly anti-Christian, pagan, and occultic which are offensive to Christians.

If Freemasonry is to be saved, a grand conference should be called in which leading anti-Masons and Masonic leaders will sit down and calmly talk about the issues and try to resolve things in such a way that everyone is satisfied.

But what if the present leadership of the Fraternity is not interested in resolving the issues which deeply offend its Christian members? The leadership should be changed. But what if this cannot be done? Then the Christians must leave the Craft. On this point there can be no middle ground. Either Masonry will change or Christians must leave it.

Notes

Chapter 1—Opening Principles

1. Albert Mackey, *An Encyclopedia of Freemasonry* (New York: Masonic History Co., 1921), I:66.
2. A. S. Macbride, *Speculative Masonry* (Richmond, VA: Macoy Pub., 1971), p. 133.
3. Melvin M. Johnson, *The Beginnings of Freemasonry in America* (Kingsport, TN: Southern Publishers, 1934), p. vi.
4. Ibid., p. 20.
5. Ibid., p. 21.
6. Delmar D. Darrah, *History and Evolution of Freemasonry* (Chicago: Charles T. Powner Co., 1979), pp. 25-26.
7. Ibid., p. 207.
8. Ibid., p. 309.
9. Mackey, *Encyclopedia*, I:66.
10. Darrah, *History*, p. 144.
11. A. E. Waite, *A New Encyclopedia of Freemasonry* (New York: Weathervane Books, 1970), II:425.
12. Mackey, *Encyclopedia*, I:440-441.
13. Waite, *New Encyclopedia*, II:427.
14. Johnson, *Beginnings*, p. 50.
15. Ibid., p. 59.
16. Mackey, *Encyclopedia*, I:160.
17. Ibid.
18. Waite, *New Encyclopedia*, II:426-428.
19. Darrah, *History*, p. 132.
20. Johnson, *Beginnings*, pp. vii-viii.
21. For details on Taxil see: Waite, *New Encyclopedia* II:251-264; *The New Catholic Encyclopedia* (New York: McGraw-Hill Book Co., 1967), XIII:951; After we came to our position, we found a counter cult scholar by the name of Wesley P. Walters who had also come to the same conclusion (*Personal Freedom Outreach Journal*, vol. 9, no. 4, Oct.-Dec. 1989).
22. Dave Johnson, "Dogs, Cats, and Communists," *The Projector*, May 1977 as quoted in *Freemasonry: Antichrist Upon Us*, pp. 31-34.
23. Harmon Taylor, "Mixing Oil with Water," *The Evangelist*, June 1986, pp. 47-49.
24. Eustace Mullens, *The Curse of Canaan* (Stauton, VA: Revelation Books [P.O. Box 1105], 1986).
25. Edward Decker, Jr., *The Question of Freemasonry* (Issaquah, WA: Free The Masons Ministries [P.O. Box 1077], 1989), pp. 6-7.
26. Jack Harris, *Freemasonry: The Invisible Cult in Our Midst* (Chattanooga: Global Publishers, 1983), see p. 152 for reference to Queensborough.
27. William Schnoebelen and James Spencer, *Mormonism's Temple of Doom* (Idaho Falls, ID: Triple J Pub., 1987), p. 24.
28. Sheldon Emry, *American's Promise: Lord's Covenant Church* (Jan. 1988).
29. Jim Shaw and Tom McKinney, *The Deadly Deception* (Lafayette, LA: Huntington House, 1988), pp. 133-134.

Chapter 2—Christian Origins

1. Albert Mackey, *History of Freemasonry* (New York: Masonic History Co., 1898), I:136.

2. Ibid., I:137.
3. Ibid., I:149.
4. Ibid., I:137.
5. Albert Pike, *Morals and Dogma* (Charleston, 1871), p. 814.
6. Ibid., p. 105.
7. Ibid., pp. 325-326, 331, 358-359.
8. Ibid., p. 814.
9. Ibid., p. 277.

Chapter 3—Legacy of Albert Pike

1. *Albert Pike* (Washington, D.C.: The Supreme Council, 33. Mother Council of the World Ancient and Accepted Scottish Rite of Freemasonry, Southern Jurisdiction, U.S.A.), p. 10.
2. Atkinson Long and Howard Collins, comp., *Masonic Text Book* (The Grand Lodge, 1919), p. 25.
3. Carl Claudy, *Foreign Countries* (The Masonic Service, 1925), preface.
4. Waite, *New Encyclopedia*, II:278.
5. Fred Allsopp, *Albert Pike* (Little Rock: Parke-Harper Co., 1928).
6. *Little Masonic Library* (Richmond: Macoy Pub. and Masonic Supply Co., 1946), V:17.
7. As quoted by Colin Wilson, *The Occult* (New York: Random House, 1971), pp. 326-327. For more information on Eliphas Levi see: Waite, *New Encyclopedia*, I:3, 180, 258; II:110, 111, 169, 220, 221.
8. Waite, *New Encyclopedia*, II:279.
9. For more information on Waite's involvement in the occult, see the index listing under his name in the following books: Richard Cavendish, *The Black Arts* (New York: Capricorn Books, 1967); Daniel Cohen, *Ceremonial Magic* (New York: Four Winds Press, 1979).
10. For more information on Aleister Crowley's influence on Freemasonry and magic, see the index listings under his name in the following books: Colin Wilson, *The Occult*; Richard Cavendish, *The Black Arts*; Daniel Cohen, *Ceremonial Magic*; Venetia Newall, *Witchcraft and Magic* (New York: Dial Press, 1974).
11. Pike, *Morals and Dogma*, 57, 77, 82, 102, 212, 221, 258, 259, 266, 267, 272, 274, 277, 278, 287, 300, 305, 307, 323, 394, 397, 584, 625, 849.
12. Ibid., 161, 516, 604, 657.
13. See Crane Brinton, *The Anatomy of a Revolution* (New York: Vintage, 1938); Crane Brinton, *The Jacabins: An Essay in New History* (New York: Russell & Russell, 1930); Bernard Fay, *Revolution and Freemasonry: 1680-1800* (Boston: Little & Brown, 1935).
14. Pike, *Morals and Dogma*, pp. 23, 35, 53, 93, 102, 105, 164, 195-196, 206-207, 223, 226, 247-248, 260-263, 274, 294-296, 368-369, 540-547, 558, 687, 688, 697, 732, 818.
15. Ibid.
16. Ibid., 65, 76, 393.
17. Ibid., 165.
18. Ibid., 200, 266, 267, 303.
19. Ibid., 536.
20. Ibid., 252, 398ff., 436-441, 520, 533, 537, 538.
21. Ibid., 252, 437, 488ff., 511.
22. Ibid., 277.
23. Ibid., 730-731.
24. Quoted in Allsopp, *Albert Pike*, p. 167.
25. Albert Pike, *Lectures of the Arya* (Louisville: Standard Pub. Co., 1930), p. 1.
26. Ibid., p. 72.
27. Albert Pike, *Irano-Aryan Faith and Doctrine as Contained in the Zend-Avesta* (Louisville: Standard Pub. Co., 1924), p. 37.

Chapter 4—Pagan Origins
1. Mackey, *History*, I:vi.
2. Ibid., I:viii.
3. Ibid.
4. Ibid., I:185-186.
5. Johnson, *Beginnings*, p. 24.
6. Darrah, *History*, p. 27.
7. Ibid., p. 28.
8. Ibid., p. 31.
9. Ibid., p. 36.
10. J. W. Mitchel, *The History of Masonry* (n.p. 1871).
11. H. L. Haywood, *More About Masonry* (Macoy Pub. Co., Richmond, VA, 1948), p. 4.
12. Ibid., p. 9.

Chapter 5—Historical Origins
1. Mackey, *History*, IV:890-891.
2. Ibid., IV:897.
3. Ibid., IV:899.
4. Mackey, *Encyclopedia*, I:314.
5. Darrah, *History*, p. 96.
6. Mackey, *Encyclopedia*, I:58.
7. Mackey, *History*, I:188-189.
8. Haywood, *More About Masonry*, p. 10.
9. Douglas Knoop and G. P. Jones, *An Introduction to Freemasonry* (Manchester, England: Manchester University Press, 1937), p. 69.
10. Pike's statement can be found on page 1 of vol. I in his unpublished work on Symbolism which is in The House of the Temple, Washington, D.C.
11. Waite, *New Encyclopedia*, I:297.
12. *The New Catholic Encyclopedia*, VI:136.
13. W. H. Rylands, Ars Quatuor Coronatorum, Transactions of Quatuor Coronati Lodge of Research (N. 2076, London), vol. viii, p. 84.
14. For examples where the swastika was used as a Masonic-symbol see: Higgins, *Anacalypis*, p. 304; Pike, *Morals and Dogma*, p. 292; Hall, *The Secret Teachings of All Ages*, p. CXCIII.
15. For phallic symbolism see: Mackey, *Encyclopedia*, II:560, 565, 573; Pike, *Morals and Dogma*, pp. 401-402, 412-413.
16. One such writer is Hall; see *The Secret Teachings of All Ages*, pp. XCIII–XCVI.

Chapter 6—Conspiracy Theories
1. Mackey, *History*, II:289.
2. John Fitzpatrick, ed., *The Writings of Washington* (DC: U.S. Printing Office, 1941), vol. 36, p. 453.
3. Ibid., pp. 518-519.
4. Pike, *Morals and Dogma*, p. 840.
5. Mackey, *Encyclopedia*, II:639ff.
6. F. Castells, *Our Ancient Brethren: The Originators of Freemasonry* (London: A. Lewis, 1932), p. 8.
7. Ibid., p. 74.
8. Ibid., p. 9.
9. Ibid., p. 74.
10. For more information on the Rosicrucians see: *The Encyclopedia Britannica*, vol. 19, pp. 559-560; Cohen, *Ceremonial Magic* pp. 104ff.; Wilson, *The Occult* pp. 320ff.
11. Mackey, *History*, II:329-359.

12. Ibid.
13. Bernard Jones, *Freemason's Guide and Compendium* (New York: Macoy Pub. Co., 1950), p. 121.
14. Manly P. Hall, *Masonic Order of Fraternity*, IV:32-33.
15. Mackey, *History*, II:354.
16. Waite, *New Encyclopedia*, I:355. For the French Rosicrucian connection with Masonry, see Waite's treatment in II:202ff.
17. *Who and What Are the Rosicrucians? Facts at Your Finger Tips* (Supreme Grand Lodge, 1938 and 1966), p. 7.
18. For a summary of these myths and the evidence against them see Darrah, *History*, pp. 378-389. See also Johnson, *Beginnings*, p. 20.
19. *Writings of Washington*, vol. 36, p. 453.
20. Mackey, *Encyclopedia*, II:746-747.

Chapter 7—Anti-Masonry Movements

1. Darrah, *History*, pp. 269-270.
2. Mackey, *Encyclopedia*, I:63.
3. Darrah, *History*, p. 275.
4. Ibid., p. 267.
5. Waite, *New Encyclopedia*, II:266-267.
6. For an example of modern Catholic anti-Masonry see Monseigneur Jouin, *Papacy and Freemasonry* (Hawthorne, CA: Christian Book of America, 1967).
7. For a bibliography of anti-Masonic books from Missouri Synod Lutherans, see L. James Rongstad, *The Lodge* (St. Louis: Concordia Publishing House, 1977).
8. See the Orthodox Presbyterian Church report found in *Christ or the Lodge?* (Philadelphia: Great Commission Pub., n.d.). The Christian Reformed Church report is found in *The Acts of the Synod 1974* (Grand Rapids, 1974).
9. A complete listing of all the anti-Masonic writings past and present from a conservative Christian perspective would take several pages. We examined dozens of such books which have the same basic objections to Freemasonry most of which are well founded. The following references are examples of what one would find in such a bibliography.

Torrey, R. A. *My Reasons for Not Joining the Masonic Fraternity*. Chicago: National Christian Association, 1910.

Hunt, C. P. *The Menace of Freemasonry to the Christian Faith*. Chicago: National Christian Association, 1926.

Rice, John R. *Lodges Examined by the Bible*. Murfreesboro, TN: Sword of the Lord Pub., 1943.

McClain, Alva J. *Freemasonry and Christianity*. Winona Lake, IN: BMH Books, 1969.

McQuaig, C. F. *The Masonic Report*. Norcross, GA: Answer Books and Tapes, 1976.

Harris, Jack. *Freemasonry: The Invisible Cult in Our Midst*. Chattanooga: Global Pub., 1983.

Shaw, Jim and McKenney, Tom. *The Deadly Deception*. Lafayette, LA: Hunting House, 1988.,

Ankerberg, John and Weldon, John. *Christianity and the Secret Teachings of the Masonic Lodge: What Goes on Behind Closed Doors*. Chattanooga: John Ankerberg Evangelistic Association, 1989.

Chapter 8—Concluding Thoughts
1. Arthur H. Sharp, "Study Shows Need for 'Call to Action' Program," *The Northern Light*, vol. 20, no. 4/11/1989, p. 5.
2. Ibid.
3. *The Morning Call*, Sunday, April 8, 1990, Allentown, PA, p. B1.
4. Ibid., p. B2.

Bibliography of Masonic Books

Albert Pike, Centenary Souvenir of His Birth, 1809–1909. Supreme Council, Southern Jurisdiction, 1909.

Allsopp, Fred. W. *Albert Pike*. Little Rock: Parke-Harper Co., 1928.

Anderson, James. *The Constitutions of the Freemasons*. 1723.

Baird, George W. *Great American Masons*. 1924.

Barry, John W. *Masonry and the Flag*. 1924.

Barrett, M. J. *Masonic Catch-E-Kizm*. 1960.

———. *The Starlight Catechism*. 1960.

Bell, F. A. *The Order of the Eastern Star*. Chicago: Ezra A. Cook Pub. Co., 1988.

Blanchard, J. *Scottish Rite Masonry Illustrated*. Chicago: Charles T. Powner Co., 1944, vols. I, II.

Boyden, William L. *Bibliography of the Writings of Albert Pike*. DC: 1921.

Brown, Walter Lee. "Albert Pike," 4 vols. (unpublished doctoral dissertation). Austin, TX: University of Texas, 1955.

Castells, F. *Our Ancient Brethren: The Originator of Freemasonry*. London: A. Lewis, 1932.

Cerza, Alphonse. *Anti-Masonry*. St. Louis: Missouri Lodge of Research, 1962.

———. *The Courts and Freemasonry*. Chicago: Charles T. Powner Co, 1986.

Claudy, Carl H. *A Master's Wages*. 1924.

———. *Foreign Countries*. Chicago: Charles T. Powner Co., 1971.

———. *Introduction to Freemasonry*. Washington DC: Temple Pub., 1931.

———. *The Old Past Master*. 1924.

Coil's Masonic Encyclopedia. New York: Macoy Pub. and Masonic Supply Co., 1961.

Crowley, Aleister. *Magick*. York Beach, ME: Samuel Weiser, Inc., 1973.

Darrah, Delmar Duane. *History and Evolution of Freemasonry*. Chicago: Charles T. Powner Co., 1979.

Douglas, Francis W. Address delivered at the Memorial Service, House of the Temple, Washington, D.C., on Oct. 16, 1977.

Evans, Henry R. *A History of the York and Scottish Rites of Freemasonry*, 1924.

Fäy, Bernard. *Revolution and Freemasonry, 1680–1800*. Boston: Little, Brown, 1935.

Fitzpatrick, John, ed. *Writings of Washington*. DC: U.S. Printing Office, 1941.

Freemasonry. Manchester University Press, 1937.

Goodwin, S. H. *Additional Studies in Mormonism and Masonry.* Salt Lake City: 1972.

Gould's History of Freemasonry. New York: Charles Scribner's Sons, 1936.

Haggard, Forrest D. *The Clergy and the Craft.* Missouri Lodge of Research, 1970.

Hall, Manly P. *The Lost Keys of Freemasonry.* Chicago: Charles T. Powner Co., 1976, orig. 1926.

_____. *The Secret Teachings of All Ages.* Los Angeles: The Philosophical Research Society, Inc., 1977, orig. 1928.

Haywood, H. L. *More About Masonry.* Chicago: Charles T. Powner Co., 1948.

_____. *The Great Teachings of Masonry.* Chicago: Charles T. Powner Co., 1986, orig. 1921.

Herner, Russell A. *Stonehenge: An Ancient Masonic Temple.* Chicago: Charles T. Powner Co., 1979.

Hickox, Norman B. *The Twelve Treasured Times of Freemasonry.* Evanston, IL: Evanston Temple Topics, 1938.

Higgens, Godfrey. *Anacalypsis.* London: J. Burns, 1874.

History of the Order of the Eastern Star. General Council, 1989.

History of the Morgan Abduction. Chicago: Ezra A. Cook Pub., Co., 1965.

Hogan, Mervin B. *Mormonism and Freemasonry.* 1946.

Horne, Alex. *Sources of Masonic Symbolism.* Chicago: Charles T. Powner Co., 1981.

Hunter, C. Bruce. *Masonic Dictionary.* Richmond, VA: Macoy Pub. and Masonic Supply Co., Inc., 1986.

Johnson, Melvin M. *The Beginnings of Freemasonry in America.* Kingsport, TN: Southern Pub., Inc., 1924.

Jones, Bernard E. *Freemason's Guide and Compendium.* New York: Macoy Pub., 1950; *Little Masonic Library.* 5 vols. Richmond, VA: Macoy Pub. and Masonic Supply Co., 1977.

Knights of Pythias. Chicago: Ezra A. Cook, 1914.

Knoop, Douglas, et al. Early Masonic Pamphlets. Manchester University Press, 1945.

Macbride, A. S. *Speculative Masonry.* Chicago: Charles T. Powner, 1971, orig. 1921.

Mackey, Albert and Pike, Albert. *Addresses.* Sunbury Print, 1871.

Mackey, Albert. *A Lexicon of Freemasonry.* Philadelphia: Moss and Bros., 1855.

————. *An Encyclopedia of Freemasonry.* New York: The Masonic History Co., 1921, 2 vols.

————. *Jurisprudence of Freemasonry.* Chicago: Charles T. Powner Co., 1947.

————. *The History of Freemasonry.* 7 vols. New York: The Masonic History Co., 1898.

Macoy, Robert. *Adoptive Rite Ritual.* Chicago: Ezra A. Cook Pub. Co., 1982.

McGavin, E. Cecil. *Mormonism and Masonry.* Salt Lake City: Bookcraft Pub., 1950.

Mitchel, J. W. *The History of Masonry.* 1871.

Morgan, Wm. *Freemasonry Exposed.* Chicago: Charles T. Powner Co., 1986.

Morse, Sidney. *Freemasonry in the American Revolution.* 1926.

————. *Masonic Textbook for Use of the Lodges in West Virginia.* The Grand Lodge, 1919.

The Mystic Shrine: An Illustrated Ritual of the Ancient Arabic Order: Nobles of the Mystic Shrine. Chicago: Ezra A. Cook Pub. Co., 1975.

Newton, Joseph Fort. *Modern Masonry.* 1946.

————. *The Great Light in Masonry.* 1924.

————. *The Three Degrees and Great Symbols of Masonry.* 1924.

Ogelvie, E. E. *Freemason's Royal Arch Guide.* Chicago: Charles T. Powner Co., 1978.

Palmer, John C. *The Morgan Affair and Anti-Masonry.* 1946.

Patterson, C. E. *One Hundred and Sixty Questions and Answers.* Philadelphia: Holman Co., 1935.

Percival, Harold W. *Masonry and Its Symbols.* Chicago: Charles T. Powner Co., 1952.

Perkins, Lynn F. *Masonry in the New Age.* Lakemont, GA: CSA Press, Pub., 1971.

Pierson, A. T. C. and Steinbrenner, Godfrey W. *The Tradition, Origin and Early History of Freemasonry.* New York: Anderson and Co., 1865.

Pike, Albert. *A Letter Touching Masonic Symbolism.* Nov. 8, 1889.

————. *Autobiography.*

————. *Extract from a Letter to Dr. Aiken.* 1884.

————. *Hymns to the Gods.* Little Rock: 1916 by Allsopp from orig. 1899.

————. *Indo-Aryan Deities and Worship as Contained in the Reg-Veda.* Louisville: Standard Pub. Co., 1930, orig. 1872.

————. *Iran-Aryan Faith and Doctrine as Contained in the Zend-Avesta*. Standard Pub. Co., 1924, orig. 1874.

———— (alias Sam Bannacle). *Lays of the Humbugger*. Little Rock: 1836.

————. *Lectures of the Aryan*. Louisville: Standard Pub. Co., 1936.

————. *Masonic Baptism: Reception of a Louveteau: Adoption*. Supreme Council, 1871.

————. *Materials for the History of Freemasonry in France and Elsewhere on the Continent of Europe, from 1718–1859*. 6 vols.

————. *The Meaning of Masonry*. 1858.

————. *Morals and Dogma*. DC: House of the Temple, 1969.

————. *Second Lectures on Masonic Symbolism*.

————. *Symbolism*. Vol. I.

Pleasner, Shireley. *Symbolism of the Eastern Star*. Chicago: Charles T. Powner Co., 1956.

Pound, Roscoe. *Masonic Jurisprudence*. 1919.

Ravenscraft, William. *The Comacines*. Richmond, VA: Macoy Pub. Co., 1946.

Revised Odd Fellowship Illustrated. Chicago: Ezra A. Cook Pub. Co., 1911.

The Ritual: National Imperial Court of the Daughters of Isis. Chicago: Ezra A. Cook Pub. Co., n.d.

Ronayne, Edmond. *Ronayne's Handbook of Freemasonry*. Ezra A. Cook Pub. Co., 1988.

Roth, Phillip. *Masonry in the Formation of Our Government*. 1927.

The Secret Ritual of the Secret Work of the Fraternal Degree, Queen Esther Degree and Sphinx Degree of the Ancient Arabic Order of the Daughter of the Sphinx. Chicago: Ezra A. Cook Pub. Co., 1983.

Secret Societies Illustrated. Chicago: Ezra A. Cook Pub. Co., n.d.

Shepherd, Silas H. *The Landmark of Freemasonry*. 2 vols. The Masonic Service Association, 1924.

Steinmetz, George H. *Freemasonry: Its Hidden Message*. Chicago: Charles T. Powner Co., 1976.

Tatsch, J. Hugo. *The Facts About George Washington as a Freemason*. New York: Macoy, 1929.

Taylor, Thomas. *The Eleusinian and Bacchic Mysteries*. New York: J. W. Bouton, 1875.

Voorhis, Harold Van Buran. *The Eastern Star: The Evolution from Rite to an Order*. Chicago: Charles T. Powner Co., 1976.

————. *What Really Happened to William Morgan?* 1946.

Waite, Arthur Edward. *A New Encyclopedia of Freemasonry*. New York: Weathervane Books, 1970.

Ward, J. S. M. *Who Was Hiram Abiff?* Chicago: Charles T. Powner Co., 1986.

Wilmshurst, W. L. *The Message of Masonry*. Chicago: Charles T. Powner Co., 1980.

Wright, Dudley. *The Ethics of Freemasonry*. 1924.

For insight on Islam and the challenge it poses today...

ISLAMIC INVASION
by Robert Morey

Islam—once an obscure Middle Eastern religion—has rapidly grown into the second largest religion in the world.

What attraction does Islam hold for its followers? What part does it play in shaping the outlook and attitudes of nearly one billion people?

Noted author Robert Morey, one of Christianity's clearest communicators on Muslim belief, compares the Bible and the Koran, Jesus and Mohammed, God and Allah. He explores the history and customs of Islam and reveals Muslim teaching about current issues such as religious freedom and the role of women.

Dear Reader:

We would appreciate hearing from you regarding this Harvest House nonfiction book. It will enable us to continue to give you the best in Christian publishing.

1. What most influenced you to purchase *The Truth About Masons*?
   - [ ] Author
   - [ ] Subject matter
   - [ ] Backcover copy
   - [ ] Recommendations
   - [ ] Cover/Title
   - [ ] _____

2. Where did you purchase this book?
   - [ ] Christian bookstore
   - [ ] General bookstore
   - [ ] Department store
   - [ ] Grocery store
   - [ ] Other

3. Your overall rating of this book:
   - [ ] Excellent   [ ] Very good   [ ] Good   [ ] Fair   [ ] Poor

4. How likely would you be to purchase other books by this author?
   - [ ] Very likely
   - [ ] Somewhat likely
   - [ ] Not very likely
   - [ ] Not at all

5. What types of books most interest you?
   (check all that apply)
   - [ ] Women's Books
   - [ ] Marriage Books
   - [ ] Current Issues
   - [ ] Self Help/Psychology
   - [ ] Bible Studies
   - [ ] Fiction
   - [ ] Biographies
   - [ ] Children's Books
   - [ ] Youth Books
   - [ ] Other _____

6. Please check the box next to your age group.
   - [ ] Under 18
   - [ ] 18-24
   - [ ] 25-34
   - [ ] 35-44
   - [ ] 45-54
   - [ ] 55 and over

Mail to: Editorial Director
Harvest House Publishers
1075 Arrowsmith
Eugene, OR 97402

Name _____

Address _____

City _____ State _____ Zip _____

**Thank you for helping us to help you
in future publications!**